EXPLORING SAXON AND NORMAN ENGLAND

EXPLORING SAXON AND NORMAN ENGLAND

P. J. Helm

ROBERT HALE · LONDON

ISBN 0 7091 5757 6

Robert Hale Limited
Clerkenwell House
Clerkenwell Green
London EC1

Printed in Great Britain by
Clarke, Doble & Brendon Limited
Plymouth

For as Geography without History seemeth a carkasse without motion, so History without Geography wandreth as a Vagrant without a certaine habitation.

Captain John Smith,
Generall Historie of Virginia

To
Jack and Nora

CONTENTS

ILLUSTRATIONS

INTRODUCTION

This book has been written to bridge a gap, the gap between a site and its historical setting. Guide books have to assume that a visitor already understands the historical situation with which a place is contemporary, while historical accounts have not the space to set up the architectural scenery against which the events which they recount took place.

Here the aim is to describe for the non-specialist some of the most important remains surviving from the period 400–1189 and to relate these to their own days. The text details many of the sites, provides lists of others worth visiting, and gives directions how all can be reached. As in its two predecessors, the book refers to the old county divisions, since the majority of maps and references which readers might wish to consult were printed before the new boundaries were set up. Over two hundred sites are listed and the majority of them have been examined. Most are open to the public, but permission should of course be obtained before visiting those on private property.

The area covered is, of necessity, primarily that of the Saxon and Norman kingdoms of England, but references to places in Wales and southern Scotland have been included wherever possible. In addition the position of a number of sites in France is given. This is perhaps a novelty, but the Norman rulers of England were also heavily involved in France, and English architecture owed much to French prototypes.

The historical notes provide, I hope, if not a complete film at least a useful selection of stills from the continuing drama to which the sites themselves formed the background, making it possible to explore England not only in space but also in time.

I

THE BRITISH RESISTANCE
400—633

1   *Celtic Britain*

At the end of the fourth century Rome, under increasing bar-
barian pressure, was forced to cut her losses. There were no
longer enough troops to go round. Something must be jettisoned
and this island was expendable. By 406 there was only a handful of soldiers left in Britain and in that year these heard that
the barbarians had broken through on the apparently impreg-
nable Rhine frontier, crossing when the river was frozen, and
were now threatening the whole of Gaul. Having no desire to
be cut off, the soldiers chose a leader of their own and retired
across the Channel.

For more than a century Britain had herself been suffering
raiders—Irish from the west, Picts from the north, Germans
from across the North Sea. Now civilian officials—Romano-
British not Roman—"took up arms" as was later reported on
the Continent, by Zosimus, "and, braving danger for their own
independence, freed their cities from the barbarians threatening
them". At the same time they appealed directly to Rome. The
Emperor Honorius replied that they must rely on their own
strength. He was himself in danger and a few months later
Rome was sacked by the Visigoths.

The year in which this exchange took place (410) has often
been regarded as the date marking the end of Roman Britain,
but in fact there was no sudden withdrawal leaving helpless
civilians exposed to death or slavery in a province deserted by
Rome. The legions had already gone in dribs and drabs over the
preceding half century. What was now happening was a break-
down in the apparatus of central government, an apparatus that
was never repaired.

13

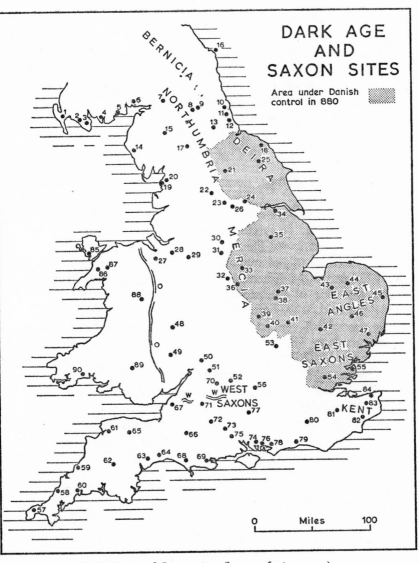

Dark Age and Saxon sites (key on facing page).

Instead of the dramatic disaster of a single year, the new picture is a more interesting one, that of the gradual disappearance of Romano-British civilization over a period of almost two centuries. There is no terminus, instead the Roman influence vanishes imperceptibly, like the Cheshire cat. One can regard the period equally well as a Roman epilogue or a Saxon prologue. Gradually the great roads break down into discontinuous sections and as they do so subsistence agriculture becomes all that is possible. The villa economy collapses and men dig holes in the mosaic floors, while in the towns the market-places turn into huge rubbish dumps, never cleared and surrounded by half-empty slums.

At first it had seemed that the Romano-British attempt to 'go it alone' would be successful. The next twenty years were ones of prosperity. Town life continued, as did the local administration based on it, and communications with Gaul were reopened, St Germanus the Bishop of Auxerre paying two visits. However, by the time of the second of these visits, the situation had deteriorated. It was probably in 446 that a last effort was made to re-establish contact with Rome by an appeal to which, a century later, was given the impressive title "the groans of the Britons" by Gildas, and which lamented "the barbarians drive us to the sea; the sea throws us back to the barbarians: two forms of death face us, we are either slaughtered or drowned". There was no reply from Rome.

The barbarians referred to were German mercenary soldiers. The Romans had placed German auxiliaries on Hadrian's Wall in the third century and established German allies on the east coast a hundred years later. Now Vortigern, the ruler of south-east England, had invited Saxon mercenaries to settle in Kent.

There was a vast difference between barbarians controlled by Rome and barbarians more powerful than their employer. At first all went well, but after ten years or so, about 440, these Saxons rebelled and encouraged their friends on the Continent to come over and join them in a land that was, comparatively speaking, flowing with milk and honey. Soon they were established in Kent, Sussex and the Isle of Wight. The new men, it is recorded, "brought by the strength of oarsmen and the blowing wind, broke through the boundaries and spread slaughter on every side", and the *Gallic Chronicle* states that "Britain long troubled by various happenings and disasters passed under the authority of the Saxons".

Not for long. The Britons fought back and now there half-emerges from the mists the ambiguous figure of Ambrosius Aurelianus, a Romano-British 'general' who successfully resisted the Saxon plunderers in the period bounded by the years 445–475. His work was continued by a much more famous—and even more ambiguous—figure, that of 'King' Arthur. There is no doubt that Arthur existed. There is equally no doubt that he was not a king. Today most authorities would agree on a certain minimum of historical truth behind the legendary accretions added over a period of almost a thousand years.

Arthur was a general acting on behalf of the little local king-lets who were springing up in the west, a man who, as an early source records, "fought against the Saxons in those days together with the kings of the Britons, but he himself was the leader of the battles". He may have had cavalry, but if so they were lightly armoured men on ponies, not the knights of later fiction.

His campaigns culminated in a British victory at Mount Badon, after which there was peace for two generations. Centuries later the *Anglo-Saxon Chronicle* referred to the battle as an historical event "in which Arthur carried the cross of our Lord Jesus Christ on his shoulders for three days and three nights, and the Britons were the victors", but its date and location remain matters of conjecture. The date seems to lie somewhere between 486 and 518, the site is more uncertain. A good military case can be made out for the Wiltshire village of Badbury, a few miles south of Swindon on the Marlborough Downs between A345 and A419, though archaeologists tend to prefer a position a little under thirty miles to the west on the hills overlooking Bath, perhaps in the neighbourhood of Bathampton.

The death of Arthur took place about twenty years later, placing him just within reach of Gildas, the only chronicler of these lost years. He was almost certainly a Briton from the west, probably a monk writing at some date between 530 and 550 when, he said, Britain had enjoyed forty years of peace. Unfortunately he regarded himself as a prophet not an historian and he is chiefly concerned to warn the Britons that their sins were inviting punishment, for now "priests Britain has, but foolish ones" and "kings Britain has, but they are usurpers".

Within a few years his prophecy was fulfilled, for in the second half of the century Saxon pressure was renewed and this time the Britons of the lowland areas went under. Reverses followed one another in quick succession. Regional British forces were defeated at Old Sarum (552) and at Barbury Castle south of Swindon (556), while in 571 the area between the Chilterns and the upper Thames valley was overrun and six years later the local capitals of Gloucester, Cirencester and Bath were taken after a Saxon victory at Deorham, a few miles north of Bath. In the north the Britons were routed in a great battle at Catterick in 590 and in 616 a defeat near Chester cut off the Britons of Wales from those of Cumberland and south-west Scotland in precisely the same way that the battle of Deorham had cut off Wales from the Britons of Devon and Cornwall.

For practical purposes almost everything outside the highland areas of Britain was in Saxon hands by 600. A new political pattern was emerging, but in the north and west British kingdoms survived, at least for the time being.

In Scotland, beyond the Forth–Clyde line, stretched the lands of the gifted shadowy Picts, while in Argyll the Scots from Ireland had established in the latter half of the fifth century the kingdom of Dalriada, a kingdom which later was to expand north and east to become the kingdom of Scotland. The detailed history of both Picts and Scots lies outside the scope of this book, but it is impossible to leave them without mentioning the exciting museums of Pictish art at St Vigeans (NO/638429, on the outskirts of Arbroath) and Meigle (NO/286446, on A94 between Perth and Forfar) and the Scottish strongholds at Dunollie (NM/852315, north of Oban and west of A85) and Dunadd (NR/837936, off A816). The latter is particularly impressive, its bare rock rising above the Crinan isthmus not far from Kilmichael Glassary.

To the south of Dalriada lay Strathclyde, a British kingdom that survived into the eleventh century, sometimes expanding to include the Lake District, sometimes forced back into the hinterland, its citadel established for a time at Dumbarton on a rocky headland on the shores of the Clyde (NS/400744) now unpicturesquely hemmed in by the modern town to the north.

Strathclyde had been early christianized from Ireland and in 397 St Ninian established a small community at Whithorn where something of his work—or at least of its consequences —has survived in the remains of the small priory, once a cathedral, against which stand a few rough foundation stones. These are all that are left of the building whose white-washed stone walls so amazed the natives that they called it simply *casa candida*—'the white house'.

The ruins of shrine and priory can be reached through a well-signposted archway on the west side of the main street of Whithorn, twenty miles south of Newton Stewart by A714 and 746. On the right is a small museum which should not be missed. It contains a collection of early Christian stones from the surrrounding area, including the oldest Christian monument in Scotland, a fifth-century stone with a well-cut inscription to the effect that it was raised by Barrovadus to commemorate his uncle Latinus, aged thirty-five, and the latter's four-year-old daughter, and which begins "*Te Deum Laudamus*" a part of the Christian office for the dead.

There are also about a dozen comparatively small slabs with early Christian markings which have been moved to the museum from St Ninian's Cave. This is dramatically situated and should certainly be seen. It can be reached by taking A747 south out of Whithorn and then following the signposts—which give clear indications—down small lanes towards Port Castle Bay (NX/423356). About three-quarters of a mile from the bay there is a car park and from there an easy path down to the beach. Here the dark sloping mouth of the cave is clear a little way to the right. St Ninian is said to have retired to the spot and there is evidence that it was a target for pilgrims from very early times. In addition to the slabs removed to Whithorn there are a number of primitive crosses carved into the living rock of the cave itself.

The other important collection of early Christian stones in this area is at Kirkmadrine on the Stranraer peninsula. Take A716 south out of Sandhead and once more follow the signposts. At the end of a short deserted drive there is a little chapel with its west door glassed in to protect the carvings. These stones include one from the sixth century and two from the fifth. On one of the latter the inscription reads "Here lie the holy and excellent priests Ides, Viventius and Mavorius", probably the immediate successors of St Ninian himself.

Although of later date, two chapels in Galloway have connections with this Celtic Christianity. One of these is St Ninian's chapel (NX/445405) on the Isle of Whithorn, easily reached—it is not in fact an island—by taking A750 from Whithorn itself. The building on the headland dates from the twelfth century and was put up for pilgrims coming to the shrine of St Ninian. On the west coast of the same peninsula are the remains of a chapel dedicated to St Finian (NX/279490) clearly marked on the landward side of the coast road from Glenluce to Port William (A747) a little south of the junction with B7005 from Wigtown. Dating from the late tenth or early eleventh century this chapel, like St Ninian's was a centre for pilgrims, who came to worship at the shrine of the sixth century missionary Finbarr. There is a particularly attractive spring just within the gate.

Also in the kingdom of Strathclyde are two fortified sites of interest—Trusty's Hill and the Mote of Mark, names which refer respectively to the Tristan and King Mark of legend. Cornish and Breton sources place the Tristan-Iseult-Mark story in Cornwall, but Welsh tales imply that Tristan was a member of a Pictish royal family, so it is interesting to find that there is an isolated Pictish stone at Trusty's Hill (NX/589561, close by Anwoth and north of A75, Gatehouse–Newton-Stewart). Originally an Iron Age hillfort, the site was re-occupied in the fifth and sixth centuries.

Easier to find, more impressive, and with a superb view to the south and west across the Solway Firth is the Mote of Mark (NX/844541, at Rockcliff, south of A710, Dumfries–Dalbeattie). Turn right at the end of the village and after a short way take the footpath on the left, which is marked by the Scottish National Trust. Here again an older site was strengthened in the fifth century. The path leads through the remains of a fortified gateway and then climbs through the defences. A vitrified stone wall was the core of these. Such vitrified forts are not uncommon in North Britain. Stone walling was interlaced with a wooden framework and when this was fired the heat through the draught holes melted the stones and caused them to fuse together. It used to be thought that the process was accidental, but it is now seen as a deliberate method of 'manufacture'. Excavations at the Mote have led to the recovery of clay moulds with Celtic designs, used to cast brooches, together with Mediterranean glassware and Gallic pottery. It is becoming clear that the site, occupied during the period 475–625, was an important centre, possibly indeed a royal stronghold.

South of Strathclyde a number of British kingdoms lingered on for a time. Elmet, the most southerly, was not destroyed until 617 and two stretches of earthworks, Becca Banks and the Roman Rig, a few miles south-west of Tadcaster and east of Leeds, may represent defences thrown up by the men of Elmet.

In Wales half-a-dozen British kingdoms survived for centuries. The most important was Gwynedd established in the north-west by a warrior-chief and his band who came from the area south of Edinburgh in the fifth century and spoke a language which became the ancestor of modern Welsh. As in Strathclyde so too in Wales hillforts which had perhaps been abandoned in more settled times were now re-occupied as Dark Age citadels. They were strengthened with stone walls and timber battlements, some sort of gatehouse was put up, and the area so defended was filled with wooden halls and huts. So much has been revealed by archaeology, but if one visits these sites today what can be seen are predominantly the banks and ditches of the original hillfort. The views, though, are always fine, giving a good impression of the country overlooked by these local centres of power. To visit them is to make an historical pilgrimage rather than a sight-seeing expedition.

In north Wales such forts include Deganwy (SH/78795, south of Llandudno), Breiddin (SJ/297143, twelve miles west of Shrewsbury, overlooking the Severn between A458 and B4393), Dinorben (SJ/968758, south of A55 between St Asaph and Penarth, on the hill to the west of St George's Church) and Dinas Emrys (SH/606492, north of A498 and close to Beddgelert). This last is the most interesting. Here there have been found Roman and Dark Age remains, including traces of stone walling on both the west and east sides. It is said that it was here that

Merlin (Emrys) buried his treasure—and armour, bronze and gold-plated, has been found here. The rather obvious tower is later medieval work.

In south Wales similar settlements exist, for instance at Coygan in Carmarthenshire, a small three-acre fort on what was formerly a coastal headland, and at Dinas Powys, between Penarth and Barry, where there was both a hall and an area devoted to metalworking.

Memorial stones from a class of Dark Age remains that can be seen on the spot. These are pillars, usually unworked, with an inscription in Latin or in the straight-line Irish Script known as Ogham. The practice of raising these stones probably originated with the Irish and of the two hundred or so known in Britain almost three-quarters are found in Wales. The stones are evidence for the survival of Christianity, the Latin inscriptions indicating Continental influences from Gaul, while those in Ogham represent Irish contacts.

There is a clear pattern of distribution. The stones occur in moderate numbers in north Wales north of a line from Dolgellau to the Dee, central Wales is blank, and it is in south Wales that they are thickest on the ground, with the greatest concentration in Pembrokeshire and large numbers in Carmarthen, Brecon and Glamorgan. It is in the south, too, that inscriptions in Ogham are most common. Sometimes the stones are in churchyards, but often they stand alone on the hillside. Today important examples can also be seen in the National Museum of Wales in Cardiff and in the Margam Museum on A48 a little east of Port Talbot.

The following are among the more interesting stones. At Llangadwaladr (SH/383692, Anglesey, A4080) the stone built into the churchyard was set up at some date between 625 and 660, the inscription reads "Cadfan king, wisest and most famous of all kings" and is partly in Roman capitals and partly in the new rounded letters [uncials] developed first in Ireland. A group of stones in the church at Penmachno (SH/789505, Caernarvonshire, B4406, about twenty miles south of Bangor) includes one that can be exactly dated, since it refers to "the time of Justinus the Consul" (540), others carry the word *magistratus*, indicating at least some tradition of Roman government, while one shows a cross combined with the *chi-ro* monogram of Christ. An isolated stone is that of Maen Madoc (SN/918157, Brecknockshire), beside the Roman road from Coelbren to Brecon. Gaunt and bleak it stands in the Roman metalling, inscribed "Dervacus, son of Justus, lies here"—and a few feet away the grave was found. In the churchyard at Eglwys Cymmyn (SN/144182, Carmarthenshire, B4314, north of Pendine) the inscription in Ogham and Latin reads curtly "Avitoria, daughter of Cunigos", while by contrast a rather well-inscribed stone in the churchyard at Llanerfyl (SJ/034097, Montgomeryshire, A458 ten miles west of Welshpool) is inscribed "Here in a tomb lies Rustica, aged thirteen. In peace." The former is probably pagan, the latter almost certainly Christian.

A third area of British resistance and survival was in Devon and Cornwall. Here too Iron Age hillforts were re-occupied and the practice of putting up memorial stones adopted. In Cornwall there is in Cubert church (SW/786578, west of B3075, Newquay–Redruth) a seventh-century stone inscribed in Latin "Conetocus, son of Tegernomalus"; at Lewannick (SX/276807, south of A30, Bodmin–Okehampton) there are stones in both church and churchyard, the latter with inscriptions in Ogham; while at Gun Men Scryfa Down (SW/427353, on Bosullow Common, north-east of the minor road from Morvah to Madron) the stone, inscribed in Latin "Rialobranus, son of Cunovalus" is probably early sixth-century.

In Devonshire there is a good stone at Six Acre Farm (SX/700483, turn north from A39 at Dean) inscribed "Cavudus, son of Civilis", moved here from another site. It is on private property, but can be seen on request. At the junction of A30 and B3219, about four miles south-west of Okehampton, stands Sourton 'cross'—in fact a memorial stone with an inscription including the *chi-ro* monogram. (The letters "HLTO" are modern and refer to the surrounding parishes.) At Tavistock there is a group of stones in the vicarage garden. One ("Nepranus, son of Conbevus") is local, the other two ("Sabinus, son of Maccodechtus" and "Dobunnus the smith, son of Enabarrus") were originally at Buckland Monachorum.

On Exmoor the Caratacus stone (SS/889335, Somerset, east of B3223, Exford–Dulverton) stands south of the summit of

Winsford Hill, inside a rather unpleasant twentieth-century stone shelter. The stone is inscribed "a relation of Caratacus" —not, of course, the great Caratacus who resisted the Romans.

Memorial stones are not to everybody's taste. There are other, perhaps more immediately interesting, remains in the south-west. No one can fail to respond to Tintagel, standing on the north Cornish coast desolate and almost surrounded by the Atlantic Ocean. Given this impressive setting it was inevitable that Tintagel should be incorporated in Cornish legend and become the castle of King Mark. It is said that one patriotic Cornishman killed himself when he learned that this was not so, but the truth, if not so romantic, is just as remarkable for Tintagel is the site of a Celtic monastery dating from the beginning of the sixth century and unique in southern Britain.

Celtic monasticism had developed in Ireland as an ascetic, lonely way of life. A 'saint' would settle in some isolated spot and preach to the handful of local inhabitants. As his fame spread, other hermits and disciples clustered round him until eventually a monastic community as it were created itself. Such communities were self-governing, the abbot an absolute ruler. Life was deliberately kept hard and simple, but learning was encouraged. When possible there was a library and a *scriptorium* where manuscripts were copied, the monks murmuring the words aloud to themselves as they worked, so that a contemporary described the *scriptorium* as being filled with a sound like the buzzing of innumerable bees.

To reach Tintagel take B3263 off A39 south of Bude. Founded about 500 by St Juliot from south Wales, it developed into a comparatively large community and flourished until it was deserted in the ninth century when Viking raiders made such a site unsafe. The almost detached headland was cut off by an earthwork eight feet high and thirty feet long. On the flat summit there was a group of buildings which included a chapel, probably adjoining the shrine of St Juliot, a guest-house, treasury, corn-drying kiln and so forth. On the seaward side terraces were cut in the cliff and here were cells for the monks, the library, the *scriptorium* and the refectory. (Buildings from a different, much later, period include the remains of a twelfth-century chapel and castle hall.) There is a small museum which contains among other items pottery imported from the eastern end of the Mediterranean, some of it stamped with a Greek (equal-armed) cross, and some later very sophisticated kitchen-ware, probably from the Bordeaux area. Clearly Tintagel was economically linked to Europe at a time when, it was once be-lieved, Britain was completely cut off.

As in the other highland areas so too in the south-west, there is evidence that local rulers were re-occupying Iron Age hill-forts. At Land's End there is Chun Castle (SW/405339, turn south off B3306, St Ives–St Just, at Morvah) high on the moor-land of Boshallow Common. Here two concentric stone walls, the inner with standing stone entrance pillars, surround an area about 180 feet in diameter in which there have been found the remains of fifth-century huts, a well, and a twelve-pound lump of tin ore beside a smelting furnace. The most important site, though, is in eastern Cornwall at Castle Dore (SW/103548, between B3269, Lostwithiel–Fowey, and the Fowey estuary). Here a grass-grown bank and ditch enclose a space 220 feet in diameter, outside which there is a second bank and ditch, con-centric with the first except at the entrance where they draw away to create a triangular outer yard. Excavation has revealed a stone guard-house by the inner entrance and traces of two rectangular aisled halls, one of them ninety feet by forty, to-gether with what was perhaps a kitchen. Finds from this settle-ment are in the museum at Truro.

South of Castle Dore and about one and a half miles north of Fowey a grey memorial stone stands at a crossroads (SX/110542), moved there from a point nearer the castle. The inscrip-tion reads *Drustanus Filius Cunomori*, "Here lies Tristan, son of Cynfawr". Now Cynfawr is an historical figure and there can be little doubt that Castle Dore was his stronghold. What about Tristan? It was not till the twelfth century that a Breton poet recorded the story of Tristan, telling how King Mark sent his nephew Tristan to Ireland to bring back the King's promised bride, Iseult, and how on shipboard Tristan and Iseult inadver-tently drank a love potion and as soon as "their drink was in their bodies, they loved either so well that never their love departed for weal neither for woe" as Malory later wrote, with tragic consequences for all concerned. The Breton poem contains a number of references to identifiable places in Cornwall, for there had occurred a mass migration in the sixth century from Cornwall to Brittany, a migration which provided that peninsula with its name, and the immigrants took with them those most portable and indestructible pieces of luggage, their language and their legends. The stone near Castle Dore is the only contemporary evidence for the existence of Tristan, but by the ninth century Cynfawr was already being equated with King Mark and of Castle Dore the modern archaeologist, Ralegh Radford, has permitted himself to write "King Mark took over the ready-made fortification, which he found deserted, and used it for fencing his court".

Just across the Fowey estuary there is a stone wall with a ditch to the north, the Giant's Hedge, which runs for about ten miles from the Lerryn stream to West Looe (SW/142571–247535) apparently constructed at about this time. One of the best points at which to make contact is near its western end, south of Willake Wood.

In the counties of Avon and Somerset are two interesting settlements. At Cadbury (ST/442650), best approached from A370 about a mile north of Congresbury, there is an Iron Age fort covering about eight and a half acres which was re-occupied in the fifth century. The area was apparently too large to defend for the western portion was cut off and fortified with rough stone walls. By the beginning of the sixth century, however, these had been allowed to collapse and there followed a period of civilian occupation when these dilapidated defences shielded a Celtic monastery. This sequence of events fits nicely into the pattern of a British resistance followed by a period of peace.

Most famous of all these sites, is the huge Somerset hill-fort covering eighteen acres at South Cadbury (ST/628252; south of A303, Wincanton–Sparkford) which has been the scene of an intensive and exciting examination, beautifully described for the non-professional by its director, Leslie Alcock, in 'By South Cadbury is that Camelot . . .'.

In the early sixteenth century the hill-fort had been identified by the antiquary John Leland as King Arthur's Camelot, probably because a nearby village was named Queen Camel, but possibly on the basis of local traditions. He wrote: "By South

Cadbury is that Camelot, a famous town or castle, upon a very tor or hill, wonderfully strengthened by nature". If there were no legends before, they now proliferated. King Arthur was sleeping in a cave on the hill; he and his knights rode at full moon on silver-shod horses along the track to the north-west which is still marked on the maps as 'King Arthur's Hunting Causeway'; haystacks sank into the hillside; fairies used the stones to grind their corn. The experts smiled tolerantly.

Then in the 'fifties of this century Mediterranean pottery began to turn up on the site. Cadbury–Camelot had certainly been occupied during the Arthurian period. A full-scale investigation was mounted. Evidence for the existence there of Arthur was not found but, as Leslie Alcock observes, there are no relics of Hadrian on his wall, nor of Edward I in his castles. So any direct Arthurian connection remains an open question. But if the excavators were disappointed in this respect, they were well-rewarded in other ways for Cadbury–Camelot proved to have a history extending over four thousand years. Occupied by Neolithic settlers, it had been re-occupied in Iron Age times and again about A.D. 500 when the old rampart was rebuilt with dry-stone walling strengthened with a wooden breastwork and the south-west gate was re-fortified with proper stone walls and double doors. To enclose an area of eighteen acres with such thoroughness argues a very important centre indeed. Within the walls there were found indications of an aisled timber hall, sixty-three feet long by thirty-four feet wide, with a partition running across about a third of the way down, and probably with a door in each of the long sides.

After the Saxon conquest of Somerset—they reached the River Parrett in 658—South Cadbury was abandoned by the British, but that was not quite the end of its history. During the reign of Ethelred the Unready at the close of the tenth century, an emergency fortified settlement and mint were established temporarily at South Cadbury, replacing those at Ilchester, dangerously exposed on flat ground. There was a well-constructed gateway and fresh stone walling, together with the foundations for a church—never in fact built. Once again the scale of operations suggests an important strong-point, probably housing about eight hundred and seventy men. This final phase lasted forty

27

years and then, with the triumph of the Danes under Cnut the defences and gates were systematically demolished about 1019. So ended four thousand years of occupation at Cadbury, a site which, as Alcock writes, "came to outdo all other sites in the number and time span of its occupations".

2 The Saxon Settlers

The Saxon 'invasion' was in fact no invasion at all, but an intermittent, slow-motion affair, comparable with the European colonization of the North American coastlands. It took the form of a very gradual penetration of the interior, the newcomers starting from safe anchorages on islands or at the mouth of rivers, thence pushing inland up the river valleys and finally settling along their well-timbered banks, displacing, enslaving or co-existing with the previous inhabitants as circumstances dictated. After the British resistance had checked this movement for a considerable time, it recommenced in the second half of the sixth century and then became very much more rapid until by the beginning of the seventh century the Saxons were everywhere established in the lowland areas of England and of southeast Scotland.

The limits for this first phase can be roughly established from the location of pagan cemeteries, and the distribution pattern of some place-names. Pagan burials were usually in unmarked graves. A few have been found in former Roman cemeteries and a number in the surface of Roman roads, perhaps placed there in imitation of the Romans' own custom of burying their dead beside their highways. But most of them have been discovered accidentally as at Sleaford in Lincolnshire where more than six hundred bodies were found in the early nineteenth century when the Great Northern Railway was constructing Sleaford Station. At the time the burials were thought to date from the sixteenth-century Pilgrimage of Grace.

The pagan Saxons practised both inhumation and cremation and there was usually something in the shape of grave goods, but often nothing very elaborate—at one place only a few eggs. There is no evidence of burial rites, though at one site it is clear that a woman had been thrown on top of the corpse and buried alive. When these pagan burials are plotted on a map almost all of them are found to lie in the lowland zone, roughly south and east of a line running from Flamborough Head by way of York and the Peak District to Portland Bill on the Dorset coast.

Another line of approach to the problem of early Saxon settlement is by way of the distribution of place-names. Saxon settlements have Saxon names, for the new men took almost nothing from the Celts. Their attitude to the latter is clearly shown by the fact that the Saxon word for a Briton came to mean also a slave, and native place-names survived only when they described such things as hills (Devon combes may once have been Celtic cwms), valleys and above all rivers—Aire, Avon, Ouse, Severn, Tees, Thames and Trent are Celtic—natural features already in existence. (Apart from such features only about a dozen or so nouns were taken over by the Saxons from the Celts, of which the commonest are ass, hog, dun, mattock and tor.)

Yet to interpret place-names is not such an easy matter as might be supposed. It is essential to know the earliest surviving form, to make an inspired leap in the dark is no good at all. Names are full of pit-falls; thus 'kirk' seems straightforward enough, it must mean 'church'. And so it frequently does, but it may equally well be derived from '*croc*', meaning a 'hill'. Fortunately it is not to difficult for the amateur to discover the meaning of names in which he is interested. He can consult *The Oxford Dictionary of English Place-Names* (O.U.P., 1936) or for greater detail the volumes of English Place Names Society (C.U.P.) which cover most, though unfortunately not all, counties.

Early Saxon place-names include heathen names such as those referring to the gods Woden (Wednesbury) and Thunor (Thunderfield) and the heathen site Harrow. Names ending with *ing* (followers of) are early, while those ending in -*ing* compounded with -*ham* (home) or -*ton* (village) are later. The -*ing* names are especially thick on the ground in Norfolk, Suffolk, Essex and Surrey. The chronological succession is not quite so water-tight as used to be thought but the pattern is similar to that provided by the jewellery and the cemeteries. Once again the names follow the valleys, once again they thin out from east to west.

Written records of the settlement exist in the *Anglo-Saxon*

Chronicle and Bede's *Ecclesiastical History of the English Nation*. Composed two or three hundred years after the events they are describing, they nevertheless provide valuable information.

The final picture that emerges from all these various sources is as follows. The new men came from north-west Europe, from the coasts of what are now Denmark, West Germany and Holland and consisted of three groups which Bede calls "the three most powerful German peoples, the Saxons, the Angles and the Jutes". They were, however, already losing many of their distinctive characteristics and for most purposes it is convenient to call them all Saxons. The term 'English' did not become common until Alfred's time, four hundred years later, while 'England' was usual before the eleventh century.

Old-fashioned books show the newcomers following lines that swerve across the North Sea with the ships covering the maximum distances and their crews apparently so sure of their destination that the track of the most northerly group, the Jutes, cuts across all the others to reach the most southerly point. In fact it is highly unlikely that they would wish to spend a moment longer out of sight of land than was absolutely necessary. Apart from other considerations, the ships were propelled by oars rather than sails and a direct crossing of the North Sea could easily have taken eight days, a poor preparation for tough fighting. Moreover, accurate information about Britain could best be obtained in Holland, where Frisian merchants were in touch with the island. So modern opinion inclines to the view that Jutes, Angles and Saxons alike made their way south along the coast of Germany to Holland and then made comparatively short sea-crossings from points between Texel in north Holland and Calais to the coast of Britain. Once back in sight of land they again sailed along the coast. It has been estimated that in this way a crossing to Norfolk or to the Isle of Wight would not have taken more than forty-eight hours, while Kent might be reached in as little as ten hours.

The ships were normally about sixty to eighty feet in length, propelled by about thirty oars. From the remains that have survived there is no proof that any of them had an efficient sail. Examples dating from the fifth century are the Nydam ship now in the Museum of Prehistory at Schleswig, and the Utrecht boat now in the Centraal Museum at Utrecht. Nothing so early is known in Britain, but a great ship cenotaph, which dates from the early seventh century, has been found at Sutton Hoo.

The Sutton Hoo barrows (TM/287487) stand to the west of B1083 shortly after that road from Woodbridge in Suffolk has crossed the River Deben. A path signposted to the river passes the site, which can just be seen but, since it is on private property, cannot be visited. If Sutton Hoo itself is rather unsatisfying, the discoveries made there are dramatic. The group of eleven barrows was first examined in 1938-9 and in one of them was found the clear impression of a clinker-built boat. The planks, fifteen inches wide, were lashed to the ribs, not nailed, there was no seating for a mast, but traces of a rowlock had survived on the port gunwale. The boat was over eighty feet in length, with a beam of fourteen feet, and a depth of five feet, though it drew only two feet of water. An interesting point is that the ship was not a new one, there was evidence that it had been repaired.

There are signs of other ship burials in Britain, but nothing like Sutton Hoo has been uncovered. The ship held a unique store of treasure—but no body. The value of the contents indicate a memorial to a member of the East Anglian royal house —their 'palace' was close by at Rendlesham—whose body was elsewhere. It was probably raised about the middle of the seventh century, perhaps to commemorate King Aethelhere, who died in battle in the north of England in 654.

The contents ranged from domestic utensils to royal regalia. The excavators were surprised by the distant origin of articles such as the bronze bowl from Alexandria, which itself contained a smaller hanging bowl and a six-stringed harp in a bag of beaver-skin, a silver dish from Byzantium, and gold coins from Gaul. There were other cauldrons, buckets, bowls and spoons, these last including two marked "Saulos" and "Paulos", christening spoons referring to the conversion of St Paul. Local products included a pillow stuffed with goose feathers and two huge drinking horns, three and a half feet long and each capable of holding six quarts, made from the horns of the aurochs, the immense wild bull that was probably already extinct in Britain.

Personal equipment included a magnificent iron helmet with bronze decorations and body harness of belt and baldrick, buckle and purse, all worked in gold and garnets—superb jewellery probably made in East Anglia itself. And, finally, there were two mysterious items, apparently royal regalia. One was an iron rod about five feet long with a spike at its foot and a stag at its head together with four projections, thought to be a standard to be stuck in the ground. The other item was a stone mace about two feet long, each end of which was carved with impassive, brooding, bearded heads. In the Anglo-Saxon poem *Beowulf* there is a description of the burial of a king with, as here, "a mass of treasure from distant parts". The Sutton Hoo treasure can be seen in the British Museum at present upstairs in the Early Medieval section and there is also a museum handbook.

The ship at Sutton Hoo provides a clue to the ships of the Saxons, the treasure throws a startling light on the wealth of the early kingdoms. Between the Saxon arrival and the establishment of these kingdoms the British had, as already described, hit back. The Saxons dug themselves in and it was probably at that time in the sixth century that they raised the grass-covered banks and ditches which run for miles across country in East Anglia.

The Brent Ditch (TL/515474) stands just to the east of A11, Bishop's Stortford–Newmarket, about one mile south of its junction with A505 and just to the east of the main road, from which point it runs rather under two miles in a south-easterly direction, blocking the Roman road, which is followed by A11 at that point. North of this is Heydon Ditch (TL/410430) which cuts across A505, Royston–Newmarket, and runs from Heydon to Melbourn. The two great ditches, the ones not to be missed, are the Fleam Dyke (TL/488601–572522) and the Devil's Dyke (TL/567660–653583). The former runs for over three miles across country from east of Fulbourn towards Balsham. It cuts across A11 (Royston–Newmarket) from which point it can be followed on foot both to the east and to the west. Even more impressive is the Devil's Dyke, running for no less than seven miles from Reach to the neighbourhood of Ditton Green and crossing A11 very close to its junction with A45. The dyke is best reached by taking B1102, Cambridge–Mildenhall, and picking it up north of Swaffham Prior. Here there is a splendid view not only of the dyke itself but also of Ely Cathedral sailing like a great ship across the northern horizon of the Fenland. All these ditches start at the edge of the fens, block the open chalk lands and end where the forests of the clay soils once began. In Norfolk there are two earthworks, apparently of the same age and raised for the same purpose as those to the south, the Fossditch (TL/772961–755874) and the Bichamditch (TF/749129–740064). The former lies close to A134, Thetford–King's Lynn, on its south side, while the latter (on some maps labelled 'Devil's Dyke') cuts A1122 between Downham Market and Swaffham, at which point it is best seen.

The extent of these earthworks and the massive construction of the Fleam Dyke and the Cambridgeshire Devil's Dyke in particular, indicate remarkable powers of organization and also the strength of the native resistance, but it was the Saxons who triumphed in the end.

Their triumph resulted in the establishment of a number of independent, often antagonistic, English states. North of the Humber were Deira and Bernicia. The former was based on the Yorkshire Wolds and probably owed its origin to the German mercenaries who were stationed there in late Roman times. Bernicia, on the other hand, was the creation of a relatively small number of Anglian invaders who ruled a largely native population from their centre at Bamburgh on the coast about twelve miles north of Alnwick. After a complicated rivalry, Bernicia eventually absorbed Deira and in doing so created the great kingdom of Northumbria which stretched from the Humber to the Forth and from the Solway to the Mersey, the dominant English kingdom in the seventh century.

South of Northumbria lay the second of the greater English kingdoms, Mercia, which in the eighth century took the lead in Anglo-Saxon England. Expanding from a comparatively small base north-west of the Trent, it swallowed up its neighbours until eventually its kings ruled a large if rather ill-defined area reaching from the Mersey to the Wash and from the Bristol Channel to the Straits of Dover. East Anglia and Essex were absorbed, Kent and Wessex became satellite states. Mercia was never quite as secure as it appeared to be and, though its history is notoriously patchy, it seems that there were frequent if in-

c

conclusive revolts against its overlordship, and its hold was never overstrong on Wessex, the final victor in the struggle between these various English states, which established itself as supreme in the late ninth century.

The northern border of Wessex is marked by an earthwork even more impressive than those of East Anglia, the Wansdyke, probably thrown up not as a protection against the British but constructed in the sixth and seventh centuries as a defence against Mercia. It is in fact two unconnected earthworks. The earlier, eastern section is the larger, the more dramatic and the more easy to follow. It runs from Morgan's Hill near Devizes along the crest of the Marlborough Downs to a point a little west of Savernake, a distance of about twelve miles (SU/023672–193666). Clearly visible on the bare downs, it can best be reached by walking east from where it crosses the Swindon–Devizes road A361 (SU/023672) or in either direction from SU/126653 on the minor road Fyfield–Alton Priors. The western Wansdyke runs for about ten miles, starting just west of A37 (Shepton Mallet–Bristol) at the hillfort of Maes Knoll (ST/600660) and continuing east to Horsecombe on the outskirts of Bath. It is most complete at its western end, reached from the road at Norton Malreward (ST/605658), a little south of Whitchurch. East of this point it is only intermittently visible and a good map is essential.

Although, with hindsight, it is clear that the establishment of these Saxon states marked the end of the British resistance, at the time the issue appeared undecided for a little longer. It was left to Northumbria to inflict the final defeats as a series of able and aggressive rulers extended its boundaries. King Ethelfrith (c. 593–616) defeated the Britons of North Wales, first at Catterick in Yorkshire and then again near Chester. After this second battle he slaughtered, it is said, 1200 monks from Bangor who had been so unwise as to pray for the victory of the Welsh Britons. Turning his attention to the north-west Ethelfrith pushed into Strathclyde and defeated the Scots, probably at Dawston in Liddesdale. Bede, himself a Northumbrian and therefore inclined to see matters through the spectacles of local pride, describes Ethelfrith as "very valiant", adding that he conquered more territory than any other British king and that after his victory in Liddesdale no Scottish ruler ever dared to make war against the English, but Ethelfrith was, not surprisingly, less highly regarded by his enemies, amongst whom he was known as "the Twister".

The second great Northumbrian was Edwin (616–633) to whom the Saxon kingdoms south of the Humber gave their allegiance, during whose reign Christianity was accepted, if only temporarily, and who fell fighting against a combined force of Welsh men and Mercians at Hatfield Chase in the north Midlands. In spite of his violent end, Edwin's reign was reputed to be one of peace and prosperity. Bede records that it was said a woman could carry a new-born baby across the island without any fear, adding that the king ordered brass bowls to be hung up on posts wherever there were springs close to a road, so that travellers might drink from them "and so great was the fear in which he was held that no one used these bowls for any other purpose".

Archaeologists have recently recovered something of one of Edwin's palaces at Yeavering Bell (NT/928293) south of B6396 and five miles west of Wooler, about fourteen miles from the royal capital of Bamburgh. It is known that Saxon kings had royal 'palaces' in several parts of their lands, but so far traces of only three have been discovered, one at Cheddar in Wessex dating from the ninth and tenth centuries, and two in Northumbria, that of Edwin's success, or Oswald at Milfield and that of Edwin himself at Yeavering Bell.

A Saxon 'palace' was in effect a village, a group of halls and huts, including an assembly hall somewhere near the middle. The buildings were of timber and have left only their ghosts in the ground. Aerial photography showed Yeavering Bell, excavation revealed the faint marks left by the timber buildings in the soil beneath the surface. The site was occupied from the late sixth century until about 670. There were a number of structures scattered about in a rather haphazard fashion, of which three were of especial interest. One of these was the royal hall, an aisled building almost one hundred feet long, of which one end was partitioned off. It has been suggested that the second was a pagan temple which had been converted into a church. The third was the most startling; a wedge-shaped timber grandstand with nine rows of seats and at its focal point a rostrum from which a speaker might address the assembly seated on the benches that rose before him.

The third of the expansionist Northumbrians was Oswald (633–641). On the north side of B6318, the road which follows so closely the Roman Wall, there is a wooden cross with the inscription: "Heavenfield where King Oswald being about to engage in battle erected the sign of the holy cross and on his knees prayed to God and obtained the victory as his faith deserved. A.D. 635 *Laus Deo*". (The date should read 633.) Oswald advanced to the battle from Hallington, originally Halidene (holy valley) a few miles to the north-east of A68, and in the battle, south of Hexham somewhere near Rowley Burn, decisively defeated the forces of Cadwallon, the British king of North Wales, who in alliance with King Penda of Mercia, had for almost twelve months devastated Northumbria. The victory marked the final end of the British resistance.

II

NORTHUMBRIA AND MERCIA
633—800

Eight years after Heavenfield, the heathen King Penda had his revenge, defeating and killing Oswald in a battle far to the south. Penda ordered Oswald's head and hands to be hung on a tree at the site of the victory—Oswestry, Oswald's tree.

Nevertheless the later seventh century and the early years of the eighth were the golden age of Northumbria, a period described, and perhaps a little idealized, by Bede, himself symbolic of that golden age. Bede grew up in a framework of Roman Christianity, but it was from a quite different direction that Northumbria had first obtained its faith, having been converted by that same Irish Celtic church that had sent its missionaries to Tintagel, to Wales and to south-east Scotland. On the invitation of Oswald, St Aidan had come from Iona and had in 634 established himself on the tidal island of Lindisfarne. Hardly had Celtic Christianity taken root before it ran headlong into Roman Christianity expanding from the south. The latter had already been established in Kent for a generation when Lindisfarne was founded.

The story of how the future Pope Gregory the Great had seen British slaves from Yorkshire and had been inspired by the sight to make a series of rather good puns is by no means improbable. Being told that they were Angli from the kingdom of Deira, ruled by Aelle, he observed that they should be *angeli* (angels) saved from the wrath (*de ira*) and singing aelleluia. In consequence St Augustine and forty monks landed in Thanet in 597 having been sent, rather unenthusiastic missionaries, to convert the English. Progress, however, was rapid—perhaps too rapid, for though Christianity was accepted as far north as Northumbria, all except Kent was soon lost again and it was fifty years

37

before it became clear that the new religion would survive in the south.

Then in the second half of the seventh century the time came for Northumbria to choose between the two brands of Christianity. There were profound differences in outlook. Celtic Christianity was insular, ascetic, monastic, and by intention loosely organized in self-governing units. Roman Christianity was international, sophisticated and highly centralized on a territorial basis. There were other differences, superficial but more obvious; patterns of tonsure, the consecration of bishops, the method for determining the date of Easter. These differences were trivial but not unimportant for the king of Northumbria was a Celtic Christian, his queen a Roman one, and it was not really possible to have a court of which one half was observing the Lenten fast while the other half was celebrating Easter, a situation which might last for weeks—in 631 the Roman Easter fell on 24th March, the Celtic on 21st April.

In 663 a great synod was held at Whitby at which the traditions of the two churches were debated. The Celtic church was represented by the mild-mannered Colman, Bishop of Lindisfarne. The Queen's spokesman was the formidable St Wilfrid. Roman Christianity, he pointed out, was universal. "The only people stupid enough to disagree are Picts and Scots, Britons living in a very small part of two islands at the extreme edge of the world." Moreover, Christ had said to St Peter "to thee I will give the keys of heaven and of hell"—and the Pope had inherited St Peter's power.

The king was impressed. To be Roman was evidently to be acceptable, to be civilized. And anyway it would be wise to obey St Peter "or else when I get to the gates of heaven, he may not open them". Colman, defeated, retired to Ireland.

Wilfrid is a representative of the political aspect of Catholicism. He travelled accompanied by a retinue of 120 armed men and was, on occasion, carried on a golden throne by nine bishops. Even his austerities were, for those days, dramatic since he insisted on taking a cold bath every night, summer and winter, until in his old age he was advised by Pope John VI to be more careful. His career was turbulent, a complex pattern of deposition, exile and restoration.

Born the son of a landowner, there was always a certain condescending attitude in his relations with his fellow-men, he spoke as it were *de haut en bas*, and—a strong individualist—he was inclined to identify his own interests with those of the Church. These weaknesses were also his strength and Catholicism was firmly established in Northumbria.

On his death in 709 he was buried in the church he had built at Ripon. Something of his work has survived, both there and at Hexham. At Ripon the crypt of the cathedral—dedicated to the custodian of the keys of heaven and hell—dates from about 670 and consists of an oblong chamber about eleven feet long with passages on its north, west and south sides. Crypts derived originally from the catacombs and subsequently from the practice of placing the bodies of saints beneath the high altar, and Wilfrid's crypts were constructed to house relics that he had brought from Rome. At Ripon the pilgrims entered the chamber by the northern steps, paid reverence to the relics from the slightly wider western passage and left by the south side. Apart from this crypt, nothing else remains of Wilfrid's church, which was burned to the ground during a punitive raid in 948. The church at Hexham, built about 675, was described in glowing terms by Wilfrid's chanter, who hero-worshipped him. He had not heard, he said, "of any other house on this side of the Alps built on such a scale" with its "deep foundations, crypts of well-dressed stone, a great building supported by columns in various styles with side aisles, walls of amazing height and length, winding passages and spiral staircases". Yet this church was probably not more than a hundred feet in length. It was destroyed during the Danish invasions of the ninth century but, as at Ripon, the crypt survives. A good deal of Roman stone-work was re-used, some of it already carved and including a slab dedicated to the Emperor Severus. The arrangement of passages and stairs was similar to that at Ripon. Above there is also an Anglo-Saxon 'bishop's throne' of slightly later date, and a chalice (about 850) in the south wall.

If St Wilfrid recalls the political bishops of the Middle Ages, St Cuthbert represents the 'St Francis' thread in Christianity. The son of a Northumbrian shepherd, brought up in the Celtic tradition, an ascetic, he nevertheless accepted the decision taken

39

at Whitby and the condemnation of the practices in which he had been raised, but he still belonged in spirit to the world of Celtic saints. He became Prior of Lindisfarne and then in 684 was chosen Bishop of Hexham, but he was able to exchange that comparatively civilized see for that of his beloved Lindisfarne. Then, finding this not remote enough, he established himself as a hermit on the Farne Islands, isolated in the North Sea ten miles to the south-east, where he remained until his death in 687, living in a hut about twenty-five feet in diameter beside which was a larger one for visitors.

Cuthbert was buried at Lindisfarne, but at the time of the Viking raids a century later his coffin and relics were taken away by the monks in 793 and, after an extraordinary odyssey across the north country, were re-buried, first at Chester-le-Street (882) and then finally at Durham in 995.

Lindisfarne is a site to visit, if only for its scenery and for the excitement of the drive across the sands to the tidal island, since the remains are of later date. The church of St Mary is Romanesque and Early English, though there are signs of the earlier Saxon church, and there are also the ruins of the post-Conquest ruined Benedictine abbey of St Peter. In the small museum, however, there are pre-Conquest slabs from the burial ground, including a number of 'pillow-stones'—flat stones, comparatively small, which carry only a rough cross and a name—and a replica of the Lindisfarne Gospels.

Cuthbert's tomb at Durham was violated at the time of the Reformation, but his coffin and a number of objects associated with him have, against all probability, survived and can be seen in the Library of Durham Cathedral, the most personal of all seventh-century remains in Britain.

Cuthbert's tomb was opened by the cathedral authorities on 17th May 1827. They found a coffin inside which were the bones of Cuthbert, a portable altar, a pectoral cross and a comb. The coffin is of oak and on its lid is cut the figure of Christ with His right hand raised in blessing and His left hand holding a book. Along the sides and ends of the coffin are engraved the Virgin and Child, Evangelists, Apostles, archangels and angels, the style of the figures showing the influence of Continental examples. The portable altar is a tiny block of oak, approximately five inches square, dedicated to St Peter and enclosed in a silver shrine, perhaps added after Cuthbert's death. The pectoral cross is also small, only about two inches in length and breadth, and is made of gold inset with garnets and—interestingly—a tropical shell. The work is English, very similar to work at Sutton Hoo made half-a-century earlier, and almost the latest example of this style to have survived. The ivory comb has thin teeth on one side, thicker ones on the other, and was almost certainly a ritual object used during the celebration of the Mass.

The tomb had already been opened in 1104. On that occasion a Gospel, that of St John—from what one knows of Cuthbert one would, I think, expect this to be his favourite—was found lying on the lid of the coffin. It is now in the Library of Stoney-hurst College, in Lancashire. The Gospel is bound in red leather made from the skin of an African goat and is the only remaining example of seventh-century Saxon binding.

In the Cathedral Library at Durham there are also two pieces of English embroidery from Cuthbert's tomb, removed in 1827. They consist of a portion of a stole about six feet long and a little under two and a half inches wide and a maniple of the same width and rather over two feet in length. An inscription indicates that they were made between 909 and 916, and they were probably presented by King Athelstan, during the period when the saint's tomb was still at Chester-le-Street. The embroidery includes the figures of a number of saints, two popes (Sixtus II and Gregory the Great) and sixteen prophets. The design was first stitched in outline and then worked in silk and metal threads. These are the earliest examples of that English embroidery (opus Anglicanum) that came to enjoy such a high reputation in western Europe and were probably worked at Winchester. By that time Wessex had united the country and the golden age of Northumbria was only a memory. Two hundred years earlier, though, the land of Wilfrid and of Cuthbert was producing works of art and of learning as good as anything to be found in contemporary Europe outside the Byzantine Empire.

Illustrative of the high level of intellectual attainment that could be reached in the apparently isolated monasteries of north-east England is the achievement of Bede. Born at Monkton in Durham about 671 Bede was sent to the monastery of Monkwearmouth when he was seven years old and spent the remainder of his life there and in the neighbouring monastery of Jarrow, probably never travelling farther afield than York during the whole of his life. Yet within this restricted environment he contrived to produce great works of scholarship and to become the first English historian.

In fact the life was not so narrow as it appears. The two houses of Monkwearmouth and Jarrow were organized as a single community and contained about six hundred monks, forming a unit a great deal larger than most contemporary settlements; there is evidence, too, that Northumbria had close contacts with Continental Europe and that the monasteries also possessed what was for those days an impressively large library—there are direct references in Bede's works to over eighty different authorities.

Within this social structure his genius flourished. Bede regarded himself primarily as a communicator of information and wrote on a large variety of subjects, producing biblical commentaries, works on metre, on natural history, on the life of St Cuthbert, and so forth, including one on the reckoning of dates —a subject in which he was particularly interested, adopting for the first time in England our modern system of B.C./A.D. dating, though he did not invent it, that had been done by a Continental monk, Dionysius Exiguous, in 525.

His great work, though, was his *Ecclesiastical History of the English Nation*, which is more general than its title might suggest, and covers the history of England from Roman times, though concentrating on the years after St Augustine's arrival in 597. He completed the History in 731, and a manuscript copy written as early as 737 is still to be seen in the University Library at Cambridge. Bede's *History* is a literary masterpiece, good Latin and good history, and although opposed to the practices of the Celtic church, Bede shows a generous understanding of them, his outlook is in fact a blend of the best elements in the Roman and Celtic traditions. He was neither a credulous repeater of marvels, nor a mere annalist, a recorder of facts, which were the limits to the ambition of his contemporaries. He described his aims as follows:

"With the help of God, I, Bede, servant of Christ and priest in the monastery of the blessed Apostles Peter and Paul at Wearmouth and Jarrow, have collected this information about the history of the Church in Britain and about the English Church in particular, so far as I have been able to find it out from old documents, from tradition, and from my own personal knowledge."

Bede died in 735 and was buried at Jarrow, but in the early tenth century his bones were stolen by a monk from Durham and buried in the Galilee porch of the cathedral, where they lay undisturbed for 500 years until they were scattered by sixteenth-century fanatics. Today a slab marks the site.

The remains of the monasteries at Monkwearmouth and Jarrow form part of a little group of early Northumbrian churches, more barbaric than their southern contemporaries, often set in depressing industrial surroundings, but very important.

In them one can see most clearly the characteristics of early Anglo-Saxon church architecture. The church is a plain stone building, high in proportion to its size, its walls nevertheless comparatively thin, three feet or less—a useful guide in distinguishing Saxon from the much thicker Norman work; its windows few and narrow, round-headed and splayed towards the interior; with a massive doorway, usually round-headed. The quoins—the dressed stones at the angles of a building—are arranged alternately horizontally and vertically, making an unmistakeable pattern of 'long-and-short work'. Within the church there are usually two compartments, a small rectangular nave and an even smaller chancel, separated by a very high, very narrow chancel arch—another easily recognizable characteristic.

The great work on the subject, unlikely to be superseded in the foreseeable future, is *Anglo-Saxon Architecture* by H. M. and J. Taylor (2 vols, C.U.P., 1965). Like everyone else interested in this subject, I must acknowledge my debt to this production, as exciting as it is reliable. In it the authors identify and describe over 400 churches dating from the period 600–1100, a figure which is likely to come as a surprise to many people. It is true that in many of these only a few stones have survived—perhaps traces of a blocked-up window head, or a bit of work at the base of a tower—but in over 200 churches the Saxon work is considerable. The surviving examples are not evenly distributed either in space or in time. Counties with comparatively large numbers include Norfolk (54), Lincolnshire (47), Kent (36), Yorkshire (32), Sussex (26) and Essex (20).

About fourteen per cent of the churches can be placed within the period 600–800, only three per cent within the next hundred years—a striking indication of the effect of the Danish invasions —and eighty-three per cent in the two centuries 900–1100. Except in a handful of places, dates can only be approximate deductions, accurate within something between fifty and a hundred years. To indicate approximate dates the Taylors devised a code which is coming into general use and which is worth knowing:

600	A1	650	A2	700	A3	800
800	B1	850	B2	900	B3	950
950	C1	1000	C2	1050	C3	1100

Bede's church at Jarrow lies on the right bank of the Tyne, between Gateshead and South Shields, while Monkwearmouth is in Sunderland, eight miles to the south. The church of St Paul at Jarrow is dominated by a vast nineteenth-century nave, the work of Sir Gilbert Scott, which as some authorities tartly observe "is best ignored". Beyond this, though, is the central tower, of which the lower part is seventh-century and beyond that again the little chancel (forty-two feet by sixteen feet) largely built of re-used Roman stones. Over the western arch of the tower is the dedication stone. The Latin inscription reads: "The dedication of the church of St Paul on the eighth day before the kalends of May in the fifteenth year of King Egfrid, and the fourth of Ceolfrid, Abbot, under God the founder of the Church." One is reading the earliest exact date in Northumbrian history—23rd April 685. There is an important collection of pre-Conquest carved stones in the north porch.

Jarrow and Monkwearmouth were monasteries and attached to their churches were the monastery buildings. At Jarrow these were destroyed by the Vikings in 794 and again by William the Conqueror during his harrying of the north but the remains of two walls, seventy-five feet long and eighty feet long, have survived. Here excavations have revealed a hall ninety feet long by thirty wide, a layer of ash and collapsed roofbeams marking its destruction, and examples of the earliest known coloured window glass in north-west Europe—amber, green and red. (Bede himself wrote that glassmakers came from Gaul to Northumbria, because the English did not know the technique.) Near the river are the foundations of a two-roomed cell of the type in which Bede lived and died. It is interesting to note that no personal possessions have been found on the site and that the food of the monks seems to have consisted almost entirely of fish—facts which suggest the survival of the Celtic tradition of extreme asceticism. "I have", admitted Bede, "a few articles of value in my chest; pepper, linen and incense."

The church at Monkwearmouth, built by masons brought over from Gaul, was consecrated in 674 and burnt by the Scots in 1070. After 1083 it was deserted, except for a few cells occupied by monks from Durham. The west wall and the lower stages of the tower—formerly a two-storeyed porch—with an interesting barrel-vault, survive from the seventh century, the upper part of the tower is eleventh-century work. Inside the church on the north side there is, as at Jarrow, an important collection of pre-Conquest carved stones.

Other examples of very early work can be seen at Seaham, Corbridge, and Escomb. The attractive little church at Seaham (NZ/422505) can easily be reached from Monkwearmouth by following the coast road to the south for about five miles and the church has—for a change—a picturesque situation about two hundred yards from the sea-cliffs. Its nave is seventh-century.

Corbridge is on the main road (A69) from Newcastle to Carlisle and here the lower part of the tower and the west wall are early, as are parts of the other walls—in particular one should look for two very small windows, now filled in, on the north side of the nave. The upper part of the tower is late Saxon work of the eleventh century.

The gem of these Northumbrian churches is that of St John the Evangelist at Escomb (NZ/189301) approached by a lane off A6073 a mile or so to the west of Bishop Auckland on the way to Low Etherley. The Taylors speak of Escomb as perhaps the most complete Anglo-Saxon church now standing. Its only possible rivals are those in the south of England at Deerhurst and Bradford-on-Avon, but neither of these are, in their present form, so early, so completely of one period, as this unpretentious stone box approached by a lane from the pit village, comfortably set in untidy surroundings reminiscent of little churches in the dusty village squares of southern Europe. Here everything is of interest, but notice particularly the sundial on the south wall, and the chancel arch, only five feet wide but fifteen feet high, which is a rebuilt Roman arch of stones from the fort at Binchester. Beyond it the chancel is barely ten feet square. Except for the years 1863–7 Escomb has been in continuous use for twelve hundred years, from its consecration in the eighth century to the present day—an unequalled record.

This handful of churches is virtually all that remains of the buildings dating from the golden age of Northumbria. However, a number of objects, in addition to the Cuthbert relics, have survived which throw light from another angle on that very rich culture.

Of these perhaps the most accessible are the illuminated manuscripts produced in the monastic *scriptoria*. Specifically Northumbrian are a group of manuscripts dating from the period 700–800. Two of these are now on the continent. The Codex Amiatinus, written at Jarrow and sent to Rome for presentation to the Pope, is in the Biblioteca Laurentiana at Florence, while the Echternach Gospels, probably produced at Lindisfarne, were sent to the monastery of that name in modern Luxemburg, which had been founded by a missionary from Northumbria. These Gospels are in the Bibliothèque Nationale in Paris.

The most accessible illuminations are those of the Lindisfarne Gospels which are now in the British Museum, though very poorly displayed; there is, as already mentioned, a reproduction in the museum at Lindisfarne itself. Three influences are beautifully united: the Mediterranean Latin of the Vulgate is placed in a setting of northern European animals and of the abstract spiral work which had been a characteristic of the Celtic world since the Iron Age a thousand years before, while the text itself is in the clear half-uncial script which was the latest contribution of the Irish Celts. The portraits of the four Evangelists successfully marry two of these elements as the Italianate figures tighten into abstract patterns.

It is a miracle that the Lindisfarne Gospels have survived. They accompanied St Cuthbert's body on its long journey, the ship carrying them was wrecked but their wooden box was thrown up safely on the beach. They were buried with St Cuthbert's body, then extracted in 1104 and taken back to Lindisfarne. Their gold cover was, predictably, melted down in Henry VIII's reign, but the Gospels themselves survived that time when so many monastic documents were being sold for the value of the parchment alone.

Finally, in the Library of Lichfield Cathedral there is a fourth manuscript, the St Chad Gospels, a little later in date than the other three, but certainly Northumbrian in origin.

Northumbria exported men as well as manuscripts. Missionaries went to Germany, scholars to the court of Charles the Great. Of these the most important, without a doubt, was Alcuin. In 782 he left his work at York to attend the Frankish king and remained on the continent till his death in 802, being buried at Tours. There in the Abbey of St Martin he had been responsible for the development of a new script, the Carolingian minuscule, perhaps the most important contribution of Northumbria to the modern world. For at the Renaissance it was this hand that was used as the model for the typeface in the first printed books and is almost identical with that on this page.

A remarkable Northumbrian object is the Franks Casket, made about the year 700. The name has nothing to do with the Franks of history, but refers to Sir Augustus Franks, who bought the casket and presented it to the British Museum in 1867. It is a small rectangular box measuring nine inches by seven-and-a-half and inscribed in runes: "This is whale's bone. The sea flung the fish on the rocks. The sea grew rough where he swam on the shingle." On one side horsemen and archers in contemporary costume besiege a town; these are the Romans capturing Jerusalem. On the other side there are two scenes. The left-hand one is fierce and pagan; Weland the Smith holds a skull in his tongs and offers another skull as a cup to the sister of its former owner. To the right is a Christian scene; the Adoration of the Magi. The three kings approach reverently, the Mother and Child wait impassively, a huge star shines above and to make all clear the artists has added in runic the single word "Magi". Scenes, say the experts, from a universal history, Perhaps, but the strange juxtaposition adds an extra dimension, as in poetry.

Runes like those on the casket first appear in Denmark about the year 300 and were introduced to England by the Saxons. They were little used by them after the middle of the eighth century, though they continued to be employed till a later time by the Vikings. The characters were angular, being designed for carving, primarily on wood. There were thirty-one letters—essentially our modern alphabet without the letters Q and Z, but with the addition of a number of diphthongs. Runic was strong magic, the names of the letters being also the names of gods and to recite the whole alphabet, or *futhorc* as it was called after its first six letters, was itself a magic spell. About sixty-five runic inscriptions have been found in Britain on a variety of objects including coins, personal possessions and above all stones. Twenty of this last group are known, mainly from the north. Most of the inscriptions are pretty brief, the longest being those on the Franks Casket and on the crosses at Ruthwell and Bewcastle.

These crosses are supreme, rivalling the manuscripts as great works of art. Sir Alfred Clapham, a man not given to hyperbole, called them "unparalleled and largely unrepresented elsewhere in Europe in the same age. Italian stone-sculpture [is] immeasurably inferior, while in France . . . it practically did not exist", and Sir Nikolaus Pevsner, an equally exacting critic, has more recently described them as "the greatest achievement of their date in the whole of Europe".

The Ruthwell cross (NY/100670) stands in the church at Ruthwell, down a lane to the north of the road from Anan to Dumfries (B274). Inquire at the cottage on the road junction for the key. The cross, eighteen feet high, is sunk in a well below the level of the surrounding floor, sensitively placed and lit, a perfect presentation. Its arms carried figures of the four Evangelists, but only two have survived. On one of the broader faces of the shaft are panels showing John the Baptist, Christ in Majesty, the hermits Paul and Anthony, the flight into Egypt and, probably, the Nativity. On the opposite face are the Crucifixion, the Annunciation, Christ healing the blind man, the Visitation and, most beautiful of all, Mary Magdalene washing

48

the feet of Christ. The panels carry inscriptions in Latin describing these scenes. The narrower eastern and western sides are decorated with what are known as 'inhabited vine-scrolls'—the inhabitants being animals—and these are surrounded by verses in runic from the Saxon poem *The Dream of the Rood* (Cross):

> Then the young hero, God Almighty, stripped strong and
>   steadfast,
> Bold before all he climbed the Cross to redeem all,
> I trembled at his touch, but I dare not decline. . . .

The cross was probably carved in the seventh century and the detail is so clear that it must, unusually, have stood indoors. Its survival is as remarkable as its creation for in 1640 the Scottish General Assembly ordered the destruction of all 'idolatrous monuments'. However the cross was buried below the church floor by the priest and in 1887 it was recovered, pieced together and placed where it now stands.

The Bewcastle cross (NY/566746) is in Cumbria. The village stands east of A6318 (Greenhead–Langholm) and can be reached by any one of three minor roads, the first of which, six miles out of Greenhead, passes through the most attractive moorland and is well signposted. The cross stands in the churchyard, high above the handful of farms that make-up the village. Carved from a single block, it was probably erected a little later than that at Ruthwell. Runic inscriptions referring to King Oswy suggest that it is not later than about 710. Interestingly, the size of the runes is graded according to the distance from the eye. The head is missing—part of it is known to have 'come into the hands' of the Elizabethan antiquary William Camden—very unprofessional behaviour.

The north face is decorated with vine-scrolls, knot-work and runes, while on the east face is an inhabited vine-scroll. The south face resembles the northern one, but also carries a semi-circular sundial with twelve divisions. The west face is the best: at the top stands John the Baptist and below him is Christ, His right hand raised in blessing and His left holding a scroll, while His feet crush two beasts, probably the lion and the adder. Beneath this is a long runic inscription which refers to the cross as "a tall standard of victory". At the bottom of this west face is the most unusual, though unfortunately not the clearest, carving. It shows a falconer holding a falcon on his gloved fist above a T-shaped perch. The most likely explanation of this apparently secular intrusion is that this is an unconventional representation of St John the Evangelist and the eagle which is his symbol.

From where did the inspiration for the work on these crosses come? It has been suggested that they were affected by surviving examples of Roman sculpture. More likely, although it sounds so improbable, is that the artists were influenced by Coptic work from the eastern Mediterranean—the hermits Paul and Anthony suggest this—but for works of genius there is no rational explanation, "the wind bloweth where it listeth".

About 2,500 examples of Saxon sculpture have survived and quite a high proportion of these, particularly in the north, are the remains of stone crosses, though none are comparable with those at Bewcastle and Ruthwell. They are of two mains types, memorial crosses to individuals and the usually larger crosses set up to mark 'preaching fields', for in general parish churches did not yet exist and it was usual for clergy to come out from the mother church to the villages. A ninth-century life of St Willibald records that in the saint's youth it was "the custom of the Saxon people to erect a cross for the daily service of prayer on the estates of good and noble men where there was no church". These crosses are usually worked with a vine-scroll, with or without beasts and as they grow later in date the pattern hardens into an increasingly conventional decoration.

North of the border examples worth investigating include a rather austere geometrical vine-scroll at Abercorn (West Lothian, north of A904 Edinburgh–Bo'ness) dated about 680, and the Nith Bridge Cross (NX/868954) in Dumfriesshire, visible on the south side of A702 about a mile to the west of Thornhill and over Nith Bridge. There is also an important collection of crosses and stones in the basement room of the very attractive Burgh Museum at Dumfries itself; take the Stranraer road (A75) and turn right immediately west of the river along Troqueer Road.

South of the border a fine shaft from Bishop Acca's tomb at Hexham (c. 740) is now in the Cathedral museum at Durham.

In Cumbria there are two fragments at Dacre (NY/456267) between A66 and the Ullswater road A592, one of them showing a very eastern animal and the other depicting Adam and Eve. An addict should also investigate the remains of crosses at Penrith; Burton in Kendal, south of Appleby; Heversham, south of Kendal; and Kirkby Stephen, on A685 south of Brough—at this last place there is a dramatic carving of the devil in bonds.[1]

In England south of the Humber the re-establishment of Christianity was a complex process; much depended on individual rulers and the policy of one was often reversed by his successor. Nor is there any geographical continuity. Kent was the first area to be converted, yet neighbouring Sussex was still heathen at a time when every other part of England had accepted the new religion and remained so till the very end of the seventh century.

At Canterbury there are the remains of four buildings dating from the early days. Isolated and oldest is the church of St Martin, standing on a hill half a mile to the east of the cathedral and best reached by taking the Sandwich road (A257). The western part of the chancel is the surviving portion of the church in which Bede says Queen Bertha worshipped and St Augustine first officiated, adding that it was built "while the Romans still inhabited Britain". Modern authorities, more cautious, are prepared to concede that it may be 'sub-Roman', but there is no doubt that here one is standing where Catholic Christianity was first re-established.

Beside the ruins of St Augustine's Abbey in Monastery Street —which date only from the eleventh century—there are parts of three early churches, built in line on a common east-west axis; those of St Peter and St Paul, St Mary, and St Pancras. The site is complicated by the fact that it now contains work covering a period of almost five hundred years from 598 to 1050.

Walking from west to east one passes first through the foundations of the narthex (the vestibule of early churches), built about 978 by St Dunstan, before reaching the remains of the church of St Peter and St Paul, built 578–613, and consisting

[1] *See also* Collingwood, W. G., *Northumbrian Crosses of the pre-Norman Age* (London, 1927).

at one time of a nave about forty feet long, with chapels on its north and south sides. The southern chapel was used as a burial place for members of the royal family, the northern one for archbishops and the concrete cases which held the bodies of three of the first five of these can be seen. On each side an additional chapel, or *porticus*, was added in the eighth century.

About 1050 the eastern end of this church was pulled down by Archbishop Wulfric to make way for an octagonal rotunda. It is likely that Wulfric based the plans for his rotunda on those of a similar structure in the cathedral of St Benigne at Dijon, for he is known to have passed through Dijon on his way to Rome. The rotunda at Canterbury was intended to link the church of St Peter and St Paul to the next church on the east-west axis, that of St Mary built about 620, of which only the west wall is now standing.

Continuing to walk east beyond this wall one reaches the last of this group of early buildings, the church of St Pancras which dates from the seventh century. Built partly of Roman brick it is said to stand on the site of a pagan temple used by the king of Kent before his conversion. The remains include the nave, the western porch, a southern side chapel and the ruined chancel arch. Important work from these sites is housed in the neighbouring museum of St Augustine's Abbey.

In Kent there are also the remains of two other early Saxon churches. That of St Mary was built within the Roman fort at Reculver (TR/228694, on the coast to the north of A28, the road from Margate to Herne Bay). The site was given to a priest, Bassa, by King Egbert in 669 and the church still stood complete in 1805, but today only the foundations are left, for in that year it was pulled down with the approval of the vicar, the parish clerk recording that the "seaside stonework" was taken by farmers "who sold it to the Margate Pier Company for a foundation for a new pier". As the Taylors comment, this has "few parallels even in the blackest records of the nineteenth century": so much for sensibility in the age of elegance. The site passed into the hands of Trinity House, since when it has suffered no further damage. Part of an important cross is now in the crypt at Canterbury.

In 633 a nunnery was founded in Kent by St Ethelberg, the

daughter of the first Christian king. She had been given in marriage to Edwin of Northumbria, but when he was killed and the northern kingdom reverted temporarily to paganism she returned to her own people. The foundations of the nave and apse of her church, built of Roman brick and rubble, can be seen at Lyminge, on B2605 a few miles north of Hythe.

Eighty miles to the north there are at Burgh Castle in Suffolk the walls of one of the Roman forts that guarded the Saxon Shore (TG/475046, west of A143 about two miles from Yarmouth). Here St Fursa from Ireland established a church about 631. The structure has gone, but excavation has recovered a Christian cemetery, the post-holes of a building and some coloured plaster from the walls.

There is a good deal more to be seen at the similarly situated church of St Peter-on-the-Wall (TM/031082), standing alone on the Essex coast east of Chelmsford and two miles north-east of the village of Bradwell at the terminus of B1021. Here a walk across fields brings one to the Roman fort of Othona, where a church was built astride the west wall. Bede says that St Cedd, sent from Northumbria to become bishop of the East Saxons, built this church about the year 654. The barn-like building that one sees today was indeed in use as a barn until about 1920 and the blocked-up openings in the walls of the nave were made for the use of farm carts. Here again there are Roman tiles and, more unusual, Roman 'lewis-holes'—the slots into which wedges were fitted so that lifting tackle could be attached: the name itself comes from their use by Louis XIV's engineers.

Other churches of the period 600–800 have survived in the midland area controlled by Mercia, that great sprawling kingdom which in the eighth century took the place of Northumbria as the leading Saxon state. Mercia's history is obscure. That she became powerful in the land and was recognized as such by continental observers is clear, but the details are meagre. The kingdom had no Bede to place it firmly in the forefront of its times—perhaps if there were more information it would be regarded as a state comparable with seventh-century Northumbria, but as it is there remains the impression of a kingdom, tough, efficient and practical, but perhaps not over-civilized.

Certainly the first great ruler, Penda, the man who licked Mercia into some semblance of shape, was himself a rough customer, conquering the valuable territory of the lower Severn in 628, warring fiercely against Northumbria with the help of Britons from Wales, devastating the northern land and killing King Oswald, remaining firmly heathen to the day of his death in battle in the autumn of 654.

Penda had laid the power base, the superstructure was added by Ethelbald (716–757) who made himself overlord of every kingdom south of the Humber. This royal tyrant was assassinated by his own bodyguard one night near Tamworth, leaving behind him a reputation for great wickedness and an earthwork, Wat's Dyke.

The dyke (SJ/232697 to SJ/300280) protected the northwestern flank of Mercia from the Welsh. It ran for a distance of about forty miles from Basingwerk on the estuary of the Dee in Cheshire to Morda Brook south of Oswestry in Shropshire. Today the earthen bank stands four to five feet high and is fronted with a six-foot ditch to the west. With the help of the 1 : 50 000 Ordnance Survey Map it can be picked up at various points between Mold and Buckley (SJ/266632) or, more easily and attractively, at the point where it is cut by B5426 southwest of Wrexham. Wat's Dyke is an impressive feat of Saxon engineering and would be better known if it were not for the fact that it was completely dwarfed by the work which superseded it, Offa's Dyke.

The murder of Ethelbald was followed by a brief period of civil war and then a descendant of Penda's, King Offa (757–796), picked up the pieces and made of Mercia the most powerful state that Saxon England had so far produced. The impression of a 'real' government is strengthened by such facts as the contrast on the same land grant between the rough script of a local Sussex scribe and the practised administrative hand of its endorsement by Offa's court official.

There was even talk of a marriage alliance between Offa and the family of the Emperor Charles the Great and in 796 the Mercians concluded with Charles the first commercial treaty in English history—earlier in the reign there had been complaints that English woollen cloaks exported to the Frankish empire were shorter than they should have been. It was a matter on which Charles felt strongly. He had once commented "What is the use of short cloaks? I can't cover myself in bed, on horseback I can't keep the wind and the rain off, and when I dismount to relieve myself my legs freeze."

Significant is that most important characteristic of a civilized state, the appearance of a stable coinage in the shape of the silver 'penny', certainly named after Penda and thought by some to have been originally introduced by that king. However that may be—and it does not seem to fit with Penda's character—it was Offa who established the *pending* as a reliable coin, authenticated by his own name and that of the moneyer responsible. These silver pennies became the sole effective currency for the next four hundred years. At the time of the Norman Conquest they had approximately the same purchasing power as the pound in 1914.

Eccentric but interesting is the issue of a gold coin in 774, probably minted from Welsh gold, and carrying an inscription in Arabic! The blast from the great Arab explosion had swept across the Mediterranean in the previous century and by Offa's day a generally respected Arabic gold coinage circulated throughout Europe—in Gaul the exchange rate was thirty pieces of silver. Presumably Offa felt it necessary to put an Arabic inscription on his gold coins to make them look real. The reverse carried the words Offa Rex in Roman capitals, but on the obverse the moneyer had imitated the inscription on a dinar of Al-Mansur and clearly did not understand the script, which he crudely distorted.

The most impressive evidence of Offa's power is the great dyke which bears his name. The scale is remarkable. The bank is still fifteen to twenty feet high in many places, protected to the west by a six-foot ditch and running for seventy miles—a distance comparable with that of Hadrian's Wall—along a line drawn with great skill which takes the maximum advantage of the physical structure of the area. It suggests the over-all supervision of one man, and there is no reason to doubt that it was that of Offa himself. Designed to mark the frontier between Mercia and Wales, it was probably constructed about 785 when relations between the two areas were good, for it could hardly have been cut without the tacit consent of the Welsh and it abandons some English-occupied territory to them.

Today Offa's Dyke is preserved as one of the national footpaths of Britain and a description of the 'way' can be read in *The Offa's Dyke Path*, edited by A. T. Roberts for the Ramblers' Association, or more fully in *The Shell Book of Offa's Dyke Path* by F. Noble.

The following notes do no more than indicate the better-preserved, or more accessible, sections in each county. The dyke starts on the coast of North Wales at a point marked by the modern town of Prestatyn in Flintshire. It can be seen on the south side of A5151, the road from Ruddlan to Holywell, between Trelawnyd and Llyn Helyg (SJ/101790). It runs just west of Wrexham and then west of Oswestry, it cuts across the lower slopes of the Berwyn mountains to reach the Severn about six miles north-east of Welshpool. In this area it can be reached from the east-west roads B4500, B4579 and B4580, which pass through it, and is perhaps most easily seen at SD/264374 on the first of these. The best continuous stretch lies in the central section, on the borders of Montgomery and Shropshire, where it can be followed with few breaks for a distance of about twenty miles from the point where it leaves the Severn at Bullington, a little north-east of Montgomery, all the way south to Knighton on A488. Within this area a particularly fine section is that south from Lower Spoad (SO/257820) on B4368 between Clun and Newcastle, south to SO/266766, the ditch in places still fifteen feet deep. Throughout this central section the dyke keeps largely above a height of a thousand feet only dropping briefly to cross successively the valleys of the Clun, Teme and Lugg.

South of Knighton the dyke is intermittent by design, for the Herefordshire plain was heavily-wooded at this time and it was only considered necessary to block the open valleys and local tracks. From a point a little south of Monmouth the dyke took advantage of the high ground on the east bank of the Wye. Finally, below Chepstow, a bank ran across low ground to the shores of the Bristol Channel itself.

Within Mercia and her subject states there are a limited number of remains. Crosses are comparatively rare, a fact which may be partly a consequence of the later dense population. In the midlands there are good examples dating from the eighth century at Sandbach in Cheshire and at Bakewell and Eyam in Derbyshire. Sandbach, twelve miles north of Stoke on the North-which road (A533), has two fine crosses standing side by side in the town square. The taller carries scenes from the life of Christ, the shorter is said to show King Penda's conversion in 653, an unlikely event. Both were broken by religious enthusiasts in the seventeenth century, but the pieces were recovered, and the crosses were placed in their present position in 1816. At Bakewell, on A6 between Matlock and Buxton, there is in the churchyard the lower part of a shaft covered with animals and figures, the latter damaged by enthusiasts. Six miles or so to the north beyond A623 from Chesterfield is Eyam, famous for its connection with the plague of 1665. Here there is a good cross with figures on the original cross-head, and further figures on the shaft, the proportions of which look odd because the upper part is missing.

Only a handful of churches have survived from the early days of Mercia. The area suffered severely at the hands of the Danes and after the latter had been defeated a great deal of reconstruction took place in the ninth and tenth centuries. Nevertheless these buildings are early in plan.

One of the best-known and most beautiful is on the borders of Mercia at Bradford-on-Avon, on A363 between Trowbridge and Bath. The church of St Lawrence was built by St Aldhelm about the year 700. The building is high in proportion to its size, the little chancel measures only thirteen feet by ten, but is eighteen feet in height. Originally there were two tiny chapels attached, one to the north and one to the south, but only the northern one has survived. The four doorways and the windows date from the original building, though the windows were reconstructed later. The upper part of the walls are three hundred years later than the lower part and the stripwork dates from this time. Do not overlook the flying angels on the east wall of the nave which are about the same period, or perhaps a little earlier, and seem to show Byzantine influence.

If at Bradford it is the total structure that is impressive, at Breedon-on-the-Hill (SK/405233; on A453, Tamworth–Nottingham, about eighteen miles south of Nottingham) it is the detail

—a remarkable amount of eighth-century carving—which must be seen, for the church itself is much later in date, the original monastery, founded in 675, having been destroyed by the Danes in the ninth century. Approaching from Tamworth, turn off to the left just as you enter Breedon in order to reach the church which stands alone on its hill. Here there can be seen examples of at least three distinct styles of work. In the body of the church are the remains of a stone frieze more than sixty feet in length, unparalleled in England, patterned not only with leaves, but also with birds and beasts and mounted spearmen, the whole showing Frankish influence. There are also two independent sculptures, in the south aisle a two-foot Madonna of a Celtic type and in the ringing chamber of the tower a three-foot Byzantine-type angel, easily missed.

Eight miles across country to the north-west is Repton, best reached by B5008 east off A38. The builder of Wat's Dyke, King Ethelbald, was buried here as was a later king, Wyglaf, and the latter's grandson St Wystan to whom the church is dedicated. Destroyed by the Danes in 874, the church was rebuilt in the eleventh century, but the crypt, only sixteen feet wide, is seventh century—St Guthlac came here in 698—though its vaulting dates from the reconstruction.

At Deerhurst (SO/870299), west of A38 between Gloucester and Tewkesbury, the church of St Mary has a complex architectural history. The nave, west porch and two side chapels date from the early days before 800, but in the ninth century part of the fabric was destroyed—again by the Danes—and the church was reconstructed in the tenth century when, among other work, the polygonal apse was added. Notice the interior windows in the tower, the figure of Our Lady in the west porch and especially the winged angel, like those at Bradford, in the apse. The font is ninth-century and has had a chequered life, being in use as a washtub at the time when it was recovered by Bishop Wilberforce in 1844. It is a very early example, for fonts did not become general before the ninth century and then were often made of wood which has long since perished. When these were replaced by stone the base of an existing cross-shaft was quite often adapted and this is what has happened here at Deerhurst.

Close by, south-west of the church, is Earl Odda's chapel which, though it dates from the eleventh century, it would be pedantic not to describe here. This small chapel was rediscovered in 1885 when its nave was a farmhouse kitchen and it is still partly enclosed by attractive medieval farm buildings. Its consecration stone is in the Ashmolean and provides an exact date, 12th April 1056.

From the eastern frontiers of Mercia two very important churches have survived at Wing in Buckinghamshire and Brixworth in Northamptonshire. Much of what one can see at Wing (SP/880226, on A418, Aylesbury–Leighton Buzzard) is tenth-century, when the church was reconstructed, but the north wall of the aisled nave, the pattern of the octagonal apse, and the crypt are early. Notice the doorways high up at the west end of the north and south walls of the nave which probably indicate that there was once some form of western gallery.

Of all these southern churches that of All Saints' at Brixworth (SP/747713, seven miles north of Northampton on the Market Harborough road, A508) is outstanding; Sir Arthur Clapham went so far as to call it "perhaps the most imposing architectural memorial of the seventh century yet surviving north of the Alps". The church was built as a monastery about 670, laid waste by the Danes in the ninth century, and restored in the tenth century. What one sees today is the original nave, beautifully proportioned and large—it is 120 feet long—by Saxon standards. The north and south walls are patterned by great arches of Roman brick, today blocked up, but originally opening onto aisles. Above these are clerestory windows, also arched with Roman brick. Dating from the early period are the foundations of an ambulatory which ran around the apse. This has been excavated and can be well seen outside the church. During the tenth century, the aisles were demolished and the western porch reconstructed as a tower with a staircase to two floors. Although Brixworth is no longer the large aisled basilica built on classical lines that it orginally was, the effect of the austere nave and the mellow red of the tiled arches is still that of a great work of art.

III

WESSEX AND SCANDINAVIA
800—924

The future did not lie either with Northumbria or with Mercia, but with Wessex.

Archaeology indicates that the West Saxons advanced up the Thames valley while the Jutes occupied the Isle of Wight and the Hampshire coast. So far as the Jutes are concerned, Bede agrees, while the group names suggest that the West Saxons would naturally be in possession of the lands to the west of the Middle Saxons of Middlesex. But the main written evidence, that of the *Anglo-Saxon Chronicle*, composed by the men of Wessex themselves, declares with circumstantial detail that they came in by way of Wight and Hampshire. The *Chronicle*, however, was written over two hundred years after the events it describes and it is not only in modern times that history has been rewritten to suit the apparent needs of the state.

It is thought that the early history of their kingdom was perhaps not as glorious as the West Saxons would have wished. It is argued that the West Saxons did indeed colonize the Thames valley, obscurely, from the east but that the ancestors of the later kings of Wessex pushed their way inland from the Hampshire coast under a ruthless leader, Cerdic, who imposed himself by force on these farming communities—a less glorious, more divisive happening which was later conveniently forgotten.

Whatever the truth of the matter, there is no doubt that by the second half of the sixth century the West Saxons were operating from an area covered by the future counties of Berkshire, Hampshire and Wiltshire. From this base they were able to drive a wedge between the Britons of Wales and those of Devon and Cornwall and then to make striking advances in the south-west. In 614 Wessex reached Bindon, near Axmouth on the Devon–Dorset border. In 658 it decisively defeated the British at Selwood on the Somerset–Wiltshire border and, avoiding the central marshlands, reached the highland zone bordering Devonshire. Exeter was occupied and in 661 a victory at the Iron Age fort of Posbury (SX/808971, south-west of Crediton on the south side of a minor road to Cheriton Bishop) prepared for an advance as far as the Cornish border, which was reached by 682.

It was these new lands to the west of Selwood, the 'great wood', that enabled Wessex to survive. The original homeland to the east was too exposed to the attacks of its neighbours—for a time it became in effect an outlying province of Mercia—and later to the onslaughts of the Danes.

The great days of Wessex began with the reign of Egbert (802–839). In 825 he defeated the Mercians at Ellendun (south of Swindon near Wroughton), one of the decisive battles in English history for it was followed by the acquisition of Kent, Essex, Surrey and Sussex and even the temporary submission of Mercia itself. A decade later in 838 he destroyed the British resistance in Cornwall in a battle at Hingston Down, west of the Tamar.

At the same time a sinister threat was developing. After two centuries of freedom from invasion the east coast was once more being raided. On 8th January 793 chroniclers recorded that "the harrying of heathen men lamentably destroyed God's church at Lindisfarne". There, today, in the museum is a stone with a cross on one side and on the other a carving of men swinging their swords and axes in a rhythm of destruction.

The raiders were Norwegians, but in general the men from Norway by-passed England, sailing round the north of Scotland, sacking Iona in 795 and establishing themselves in Ireland, but not settling in England until they crossed from their new homes to north-west England in the early tenth century.

England had become involved in a general Scandinavian expansion as the Swedes moved into Russia and the Danes sailed up the rivers of France and England. The causes of this expansion are not clearly understood, but they were certainly powered by three centuries of ship-building which had evolved beautifully engineered sailing vessels that make the Sutton Hoo ship look very out-of-date. The most impressive survival was found at Gokstad in 1880 and is now in a museum at Oslo. It is rather longer than a cricket pitch, seventy-six feet six inches from stem to stern, with a beam of seventeen feet six inches and a depth of almost seven feet—but drawing only two foot nine inches of water, an important consideration in a raider. Its sides were clinker-built, with sixteen overlapping oak planks caulked with animal hair and nailed to one another, but fastened to the ribs and keel by ties, a form of construction that gave the ship great elasticity. It was completely seaworthy; in 1892 a replica sailed from Norway to America in twenty-eight days.

Each summer the Danish ships sailed south-west along the Frisian coast and thence down the Channel. These were essentially commando raids. Comparatively large forces, probably to be numbered in thousands rather than in hundreds, would descend on unprepared areas, disembark, provide themselves with horses, and organize lightning thrusts into the interior. In the autumn they would sail home again with their spoils. But about 850 they began to winter here, adding to their plunder in the following season, and from that it was only a short step to permanent settlement.

That step was taken in 865 when what became known as the 'Great Army' arrived. At first it moved from one area to another each year. Then in 876 Northumbria ceased to exist when a part of the army hived off and colonized Yorkshire. In the following year a similar permanent settlement was established in Mercia based on what later became the 'five boroughs' of Leicester, Lincoln, Nottingham, Stamford and Derby.

In 878 an attempt was made to colonize the last important Saxon kingdom, Wessex, and it was then that King Alfred was forced to retreat to the new lands west of the great forest and to base himself on Athelney where an area of about thirty acres rose a little above the marshes of the Somerset Levels. Years later he ordered a monastery to be built on the site and though nothing of this remains today, on the east side of the road from Taunton to Glastonbury (A361) there is a modern rough stone monument (ST/344292) while on the 'island' behind it there stands a small truncated obelisk put up in 1801.

From Athelney Alfred emerged at the head of an army to

defeat the Danes decisively at Edington, about fifteen miles south of their headquarters at Chippenham. The most probable site of the fighting is on the downs above Bratton (ST/901516), south of B3098 and a few miles east of Westbury. Here there is one of the white horses often said to have been cut at Alfred's command. In fact there is, disappointingly, evidence that in its present form it was cut in 1778, remodelling an earlier and smaller horse which faced in the opposite direction and it is, of course, no longer possible to date this earlier figure.

The defeated Danes withdrew to East Anglia, from which area they carried on the struggle until 886, when the treaty of Wedmore was made. Neither side had been able to destroy the other and the terms represent an agreement between equals. Mercia was to be divided, the boundary between Saxon England and the Danelaw running up the Thames, then north up the river Lea to its source, from there across country to Bedford and then up the river Ouse to Watling Street, the modern A5. Thence it followed that road to a point east of Wellington about midway between Lichfield and Shrewsbury. Although the Danelaw became part of Saxon England in the next century it had by then acquired a distinct character of its own, the area where the Danes lived whoever ruled over them, and today Watling Street still divides the Mercians of Warwickshire from the Danes of Leicestershire—counties with very different place-names and dialects.

The ninth century had been one of turmoil and it is scarcely surprising that little has survived from those years. Of Alfred himself the most interesting relics are at Oxford. In the Bodleian there is a translation into English of Gregory the Great's *Pastoral Care*, one of the manuscripts that Alfred commanded to be made "that he might send them to his bishops"—in this case the Bishop of Worcester. In the Ashmolean there is a more immediately exciting object, the piece of work known as 'Alfred's Jewel', dug up in 1693 two or three miles to the west of Athelney.

The 'jewel' is a pear-shaped object, two and a half inches long and about an inch wide. It is cloisonné enamel work showing a three-quarter-length figure dressed in green and red standing against a blue background and holding a sceptre in each hand. The whole is in a gold setting which includes the words "Alfred had me made". At the narrower end is a boar's head with its mouth open to hold something—perhaps a little stick, for in the preface to the *Pastoral Care* Alfred wrote that with each copy there would be a book marker, a rod with which to follow the words, and it is likely that the 'jewel' is the head of one of these.

There is plenty of evidence for the partial destruction of existing churches, and it would appear that no monastery remained to the north and east of Watling Street. Of churches that date from this barren century the most rewarding are those at Heysham in Lancashire, Britford in Wiltshire and South Elmham in Suffolk. At Heysham (SD/410617, west of Lancaster on A589) St Peter's has a ninth-century west doorway and southwest window—by themselves perhaps hardly worth a detour, but in the churchyard there is the lower half of a cross showing, most unusually, buildings and for good measure there is also a rather later hogback tomb with carved bears at either end.

Britford (SU/163284) stands on the outskirts of Salisbury to the east of the road to Ringwood (A338). The nave of St Peter's is ninth-century with a good south doorway and two interesting archways at the east end, one being composed of Roman tiles and the other decorated with a fine pattern of vine-scrolls and square interlaced work.

In some ways, though, the most unusual ninth-century remains are those at South Elmham (TM/309826) in Suffolk, just south of the county border with Norfolk and south too of the road from Diss to Bungay (A143). These are in a picturesque setting outside the village of South Elmham St Cross and consist of the western part of a nave, the stonework of which has the scaffolding holes still visible, standing within an earthen rampart and ditch. Excavations, though, have revealed no trace of any sort of floor. South Elmham was a puzzle until it was suggested that here was a church begun at the time of the Danish invasions and never completed. All now falls into place. Standing here one receives the clearest impression of work begun in this dangerous century and protected by a rampart, but brought to a stop with dreadful suddenness and finality.

Only a few individual pieces of carving of any general interest are left from the troubled times. At Peterborough there is the strange, debateable object known as the 'Hedda stone'—a solid

Helmet from the royal ship-burial at Sutton Hoo; *see* pp. 31–2
(*British Museum*)

The King Alfred Jewel; *see* pp. 63–4 *(Ashmolean Museum, Oxford)*

The Franks Casket, front panel. On the left, Weland the Smith; on the right, the Adoration of the Magi; *see* p. 47 *(British Museum)*

The Lindisfarne Gospels, the Evangelist St John; *see* pp. 46–7
(British Library)

All Saints Church, Earls Barton;
see p. 85 (National Monuments
Record, Crown Copyright)

The Ruthwell Cross; see pp.
48–9 (Dept of the Environment,
Crown Copyright)

St Lawrence's Church, Bradford-on-Avon; *see* p. 57 *(National Monuments Record, Crown Copyright)*

Church of St. John the Evangelist, Escomb; *see* pp. 45–6 *(National Monuments Record, Crown Copyright)*

All Saints Church, Brixworth; *see* p. 59 *(National Monuments Record, Crown Copyright)*

The Raising of Lazarus, Chichester Cathedral; *see* pp. 123–4
(National Monuments Record, Crown Copyright)

King Harold is killed, Bayeux Tapestry; see pp. 96–7 (Radio Times Hulton Picture Library)

block in the shape of a small gabled chest, its sides decorated with human figures. It is said to have been carved to stand over the remains of the monks slaughtered at Peterborough by the Danes, but it may be rather earlier in date than the raids. In the Wiltshire village of Codford St Peter, about five miles south-east of Warminster on the Salisbury road (A36), there is the shaft of a cross carved with the figure, unique and inexplicable, of a man holding what appears to be a mallet in his left hand while his right grasps the branch of a tree as he stands gazing upwards. In the West Riding there are three crosses in the churchyard at Ilkley, ten miles west of Skipton on A65, which like those at Sandbach were placed in their present position in the nineteenth century. All three carry figures and animals, but the detail is rather weathered and is best seen when strong sunlight and shadow give them back their original patterning. The most easterly, however, has in its lowest panels quite sharp carvings of animals in pairs. The smallest, most weathered shaft carries the figures of the four Evangelists. Also from Yorkshire, but now in the Victoria and Albert Museum, is the Easby cross-shaft with clear vine-scrolls and a splendid group of apostles' heads. A different type of object is the ninth-century coffin-lid or tomb-slab at Wirksworth, six miles south of Matlock on B5036, carved with figures from the Gospels.

In the first half of the tenth century the Irish-Norse raiders swept into the north-west, establishing themselves on the Wirral peninsula, occupying the coastlands from Dee to Solway, and crossing the Pennines to set up in 919 a Norse kingdom with its capital at York. Other bands harried the shores of Wales and south-west England, though they made no permanent settlements. In these last areas Norse names for natural features are scattered along the coasts—and a recent work on British fleas has suggested that the otherwise inexplicable existence in Devonshire of a Scottish variety of flea may be due to its arrival in bundles of fodder brought by northern raiders!

Norse power in England was short-lived, for the tenth century witnessed the conquest of the north by Wessex. Alfred was succeeded by his son Edward (901–924) and his grandson Athelstan (924–939), while his daughter Ethelfleda effectively ruled Mercia from 911–918 and it was to this remarkable family that

E

the success of Wessex was due. Edward and Ethelfleda worked in tandem and between them conquered the land as far as the Mersey and the Humber. Every Danish colony south of that line was annexed and by the time of Edward's death he had also received the 'submission' of the Scots, of the kingdom of Strathclyde, of the Saxon earls in what was left of Northumbria, and of the Norse ruler in Yorkshire—submissions that were perhaps something of a formality, but which nevertheless indicated a startling change from the picture a generation or so earlier when the ruler of Wessex was only a guerrilla leader lurking in the flooded Somerset Levels.

The details of the campaigns by which all this was achieved are not of much interest, but the means by which they were held are worthy of notice. Throughout the intention was to allow defeated enemies to retain their own social structure and to pin down the frontiers with fortress-towns.

The policy of allowing the Scandinavian settlements to retain their identity has resulted in the survival of a large number of Scandinavian place-names and also, more surprisingly, of a considerable proportion of Scandinavian words. The explanation is that modern English is derived from the English dialect of the East Midlands, which was precisely the area in which Danish influence was strongest. There is a multitude of these words in everyday use—anger, bread, call, die, eggs, happy, husband, ill, low, root, sky, take, and window are only a few of the commonest.

The typical endings of Scandinavian place-names, in order of importance, are -by (village), -thorp (hamlet) and -toft (farm). Two-thirds of the -by endings are combined with personal names and their distribution indicates the areas of intensive settlement. Over eighty-five per cent are in Lincolnshire, Yorkshire and Leicestershire, while almost all the rest are in Nottinghamshire, Derbyshire, Northamptonshire and Norfolk. These were precisely the areas which the Great Army had colonized in the mid-ninth century. An unusual group of names is that which consists of a Scandinavian prefix followed by a Saxon suffix—known as 'Grimston hybrids' from a number of places where the Scandinavian grim is combined with the Saxon ton, indicating existing Saxon settlements taken under Scandinavian control.

For Scandinavian place-names the map and lists in the Ordnance Survey publication *Britain Before the Norman Conquest* are invaluable, since the study of place-names is full of surprises. Thus 'Derby' (north village) is an impeccably Scandinavian name, but it was in fact a Saxon settlement the name of which had been translated by the newcomers, for the old name was 'Northworthy', also meaning north village. Sometimes the new men adapted the existing Saxon names to their own pronunciation. York, for instance, was metamorphosed from Eorforwick to Yorwick, a change that is recognizable but hardly guessable. The existence of 'Dane' in a place-name looks foolproof, but is in fact no help at all; thus Danescourt in Kent is in fact derived from the Saxon *dene* (valley).

When all the evidence is put together the picture that emerges is of heavy concentrations of Scandinavians in the north-west, along the river valleys of the east coast from the Tees to the Welland, and in East Anglia to the north of Great Yarmouth, from which areas settlers spread over the lands of the Danelaw. They gave to that area characteristics which survived the Norman Conquest, including a social structure distinct from that of Saxon England. In many districts there existed a sort of peasant aristocracy, the descendants of the rank and file of the Danish armies, farming land which had been partitioned during the ninth-century invasions, owing services to a superior, but ones that were not too burdensome, and it is significant that in 1086 the richest counties appear to have been in just this area— Lincolnshire, Norfolk and Suffolk.

While Scandinavian settlement was still taking place the Saxons were already recovering lost territory. As they did so they defended their frontiers and held down their conquests by establishing fortress-towns, or *burhs*. It was Alfred who had begun this policy and so thoroughly was it carried out that by the early tenth century no part of that kingdom was more than twenty miles from one of these settlements, intended to combine the functions of a strong-point, a place of refuge, and, it was hoped, a trading centre. Thirty-two are mentioned in the early tenth-century document known as the Burghal Hidage and almost all have been identified. Typically, Alfred used whatever materials lay to hand—an Iron Age hillfort at Pilton, Roman

town walls at Exeter and Winchester, a Roman fort at Portchester, a steep hill at Shaftesbury. If there was nothing suitable,
then a new site must be selected and fortified, as happened at
Wareham.

The construction consisted essentially of raising an earthen
rampart faced with turf, crowned with a palisade and protected
by a forward ditch. To each pole (five and a half yards) of rampart four men were allotted, and the defences were to be repaired
annually, work that was to be carried out in the fortnight following the Rogation Days—approximately the latter half of May.
The Burghal Hidage shows that the size of these garrisons varied
greatly, from 100 men to 2,400, and consequently so did the
size of the burhs. For there was nothing theoretical about all
this. Where the circumference of a burh can be checked against
the Burghal Hidage the figures correspond very closely: at
Wareham the ramparts when complete would have measured
2,180 yards against a theoretical 2,200 yards; at Wallingford
the embankments measure 3,030 yards against a theoretical
3,300, while at Winchester where the Saxon ramparts have
not survived, the medieval walls measure 3,280 yards against
a theoretical length of 3,300 yards for the Saxon peri-
meter.

Edward the Elder and Ethelfleda continued Alfred's policy
and between them established twenty-two burhs, of which the
position of eighteen is known, and repaired the defences of a
number of existing towns, such as the Roman walls at Lincoln
and Colchester. The consequence was the creation of a line of
fortresses running from Essex to the Mersey. At the close of the
tenth century, when a second phase of Danish attacks took place,
burh building was resumed and, as already mentioned, evidence
of extensive but uncompleted work of this type has been found
at South Cadbury.

Although some burhs were 'rotten boroughs' from the start,
quite a number flourished—a dozen of the creations of Edward
and his sister were still important at the time of the Norman
Conquest—and so it is hardly surprising that very little of all
this work can be seen above ground today.

For the ordinary traveller the most imposing remains are
those of Alfred's creation at Wareham (take A352 south from

Dorchester) where the rectangle of the Saxon rampart can be walked along the east, north and west sides. The fronting ditch was recut in Norman times. While here do not miss the church of St Martin which stands on the north wall and of which the chancel and nave are tenth century and at the other end of the town the church of St Mary where there are inscribed stones dating from the fifth or sixth centuries.

In Berkshire the ramparts at Wallingford (east of Didcot on A4130) stand ten feet high. They can most easily be reached in the park to the west of the town. Portchester (SU/625045, south of A27 in Portsmouth harbour) which seems to have a little of everything, possesses the only surviving Anglo-Saxon gateway. At Cricklade, on the main road between Cirencester and Swindon, the defensive earthwork can be made out.

In Devon there are three sites. At Halwell (SX/784532; A381, Totnes–Kingsbridge, then take B3207 towards Dartmouth, the camp lies on the north side of the road about a mile out of the village) there is a good rampart and ditch. The burh was later moved from Halwell to Totnes. In the north of the county the earthwork marked on the map as Burridge Camp is an Iron Age hillfort which became the burh of Pilton. The camp (SS/569352, east of A39 Barnstaple–Lynton) lies two miles north of Barnstaple and is best reached by following a lane from East Pilton. The third burh is at Lydford (SX/510847, just west of A386, Okehampton–Tavistock) where a natural site was strengthened. in Alfred's time by a stone-faced rampart.

Of Edward and Ethelfleda's creations little has survived. There is something at Witham, between Chelmsford and Colchester, but there are better remains in Cheshire at Eddisbury (SJ/553694) on the hill north of A54, Chester–Northwich, just east of Kelsall, where a natural site was strengthened.

Partly in consequence of this policy the tenth and eleventh centuries saw a resurgence of town life unequalled since the days of the Romans. Not all these urban centres were based on the new forts. Many represent a peaceful development of late Saxon civilization. The fate of the Roman towns, of that complex urban pattern built up over three centuries, has been —and indeed still is—hotly debated. Were they deserted, or did they survive? On balance, a verdict given twenty years ago still seems to hold good; there was neither wholesale destruction nor universal survival.

Certainly Roman towns in some areas were functioning as the strongholds of local kings in the sixth century, towns such as Gloucester, Cirencester and Bath. Certainly, too, a century later in 685 St Cuthbert was taken on a Cook's tour of the Roman remains at Carlisle by the city reeve. And it is significant that over three-quarters of the town names of Roman Britain have survived, in one form or another. As against this, the Saxons in the early centuries were, sociologically, not town dwellers. Plunder was their first objective, farmland their second, and they looked on Roman ruins as "cunning work of giants". Nevertheless as early as the fifth century they did, at York and Canterbury, perhaps exceptionally, put up rather primitive huts in line with the Roman streets.

In the ninth century the picture was altered by the attacks of the Norsemen and the wisdom of the house of Wessex, when the urban life that was just beginning to develop was greatly accelerated by the Scandinavian pressure and the method adopted to resist that pressure. As a result during the next hundred years a pattern was established which was not much changed until the Industrial Revolution a thousand years later.

Trade and defence were in many ways indivisible. Thus by the mid-tenth century there was no major river in territory under Saxon rule that was not controlled by a settlement near the coast, the passage upstream being usually blocked by a bridge which was in effect both a toll-gate for peaceable traders and a barrier to sea-borne raiders.

The enthusiasm of local groups and the mechanical excavation of town centres has increased our knowledge of Saxon settlements. Evidence, most of it from south-east England, is accumulating to show that many towns were laid out according to a more or less standard grid pattern. Through the centre ran the main street, wide enough for a market to be held in it. On either side were houses, carefully spaced—at Canterbury it is recorded that there had to be a distance of two feet between buildings to serve as 'eavesdrip'—and behind these a narrow back street, running away from which were long rectangular strips of land, kitchen gardens. The owners of these plots also had shares in the fields beyond the town walls for there was no complete separation between town and country.

Some towns were the creation of local men themselves. At St Albans an ingenious abbot deliberately blocked the old Roman main road of Watling Street so that traffic, and therefore trade, would have to pass through his own new town to the east. Such places were much less likely to have an orderly plan. Thetford in East Anglia became an important place in the tenth century, but excavations indicate that it grew up quite casually with no alignment of houses along parallel streets.

Domesday Book, the Norman inquest of 1086, records about 100 towns and it is likely that by the end of the Saxon period some ten per cent of the population were town-dwellers. By combining a number of sources of information it is possible to construct a list of the largest towns in the mid-tenth century. It is generally agreed that London was in a class by itself, with a population of something between 12,000 and 20,000. It was a long-established port and already in Bede's day "the exchange point of many nations". Until recently there was not much material evidence of the port, but in 1974 excavations at New Fresh Wharf, between London Bridge and Billingsgate, revealed above the Roman stone-built wharfage the remains of a Saxon wooden wharf with a radio-carbon date of about 760. Here a row of silver birch posts had held up a wall made from the planks of an old clinker-built wooden-pegged boat.

The wharfage at London throws an interesting light on Saxon building methods. So too does the discovery in Northampton of what appear to be three Saxon concrete mixers, probably constructed about the middle of the ninth century. Approximately six feet in diameter they took the form of saucers cut out of the under-lying rock and provided with a central hole. The evidence suggests a post to which wooden paddles were fixed and which was rotated in this hole through 180 degrees and then back again by two men, one for each paddle. One of these mixers will eventually be on view in the Northampton Museum in Guildhall Road.

Next in size to London was the northern 'capital' of York with a population of about 8,000. These two towns were followed at a considerable distance by a dozen or so places, here listed in their approximate size, which ran from about 5,000 down to 2,000: Winchester, Norwich, Lincoln, Chester, Thetford, Exeter, Gloucester, Canterbury, Worcester, Oxford, Ipswich, Hereford, Colchester and Cambridge.

Although small in population, these were not necessarily unimportant places. Winchester, the capital of Wessex, was a sophisticated centre with three churches, two palaces and nine official moneyers; it was a repository for standard weights and measures and a centre to which exotic products—silks, precious stones, worked ivory—were brought and at which a highly individual art developed, that of the 'Winchester School'. Derived from continental models the style evolved was unmistakeably original and insular. The figures are drawn with quick nervous strokes, their clothes swirl around thin twisted limbs and hunched shoulders. The whole effect is one of mobility and energy. From Winchester the style spread to other centres in the south-east. Examples can best be seen in the British Museum where the plums include the charter of the New Minster at Winchester (966), the Benedictional of St Ethelwold painted at Winchester between 971 and 984, and a copy of the Utrecht Psalter probably drawn at Canterbury about the year 1000. It was the walls which, providing security, made all this luxury possible. The *Chronicle* records how in 1006 the people of Winchester watched a Danish army "as they went past the gates towards the sea".

Trade depended, at least in part, on a reliable nation-wide coinage and minting was a prime function of many towns. The official dies were kept in London and the licensed moneyers had to go there to collect them, after which they went home and struck the national coinage locally. It was a neat arrangement and was supported by stringent legislation. In Athelstan's *Laws*, it states that "there shall be one coinage throughout the king's dominions. No man is to refuse it. There shall be no minting except in a 'port'. And if a minter be convicted of striking bad money, the hand with which he was guilty shall be cut off and set up on the mint smithy. . . ." Not surprisingly, the English currency came to be accepted throughout northern Europe. Runs of Anglo-Saxon coins can be seen in many museums. The angular heads, sufficiently enlarged, are works of art, but in general there is very little variation—like modern road signs, the object is recognition, not great originality. Twelve pennies made up one shilling, and twenty shillings one pound of silver—a pattern that survived for a thousand years until the introduction of a decimal coinage in 1971.

The possession of a mint is usually an indication of the importance of a town—London had twenty moneyers—and the names are known of eighty-eight places that possessed mints at some time or other. A different indicator is the appearance of the word 'port', which at this period meant any market town. Here local traders were already grouping themselves into guilds, something between a chamber of commerce and a friendly society—"If any member fall ill within sixty miles we are to provide fifteen men to fetch him and thirty if he be dead, and they are to bring him to the place he wished in life".

In the early days external trade was in the hands of the Frisians, but by the late tenth century English merchants were operating as far away as Rome and there was constant trafficking with Scandinavia, Germany and France. Merchants were recognized as being of considerable importance, one document recording that a merchant who had carried out three voyages at his own expense was regarded as having a status equivalent to that of a thegn. This was no mere social honour when each class carried its own privileges—and penalties.

Apart from wine, imports were largely of luxury goods: Aelfric's *Colloquy* lists them as "purple robes and silk, precious stones and gold, rare apparel and spices, wine and oil, ivory and brass, copper and tin, sulphur and glass, and many such things". Glass was just beginning to be made again in England, the earliest known kilns, found at Glastonbury, are probably tenth-century and it was at about this time too that native glazed pottery made its appearance.

Exports were mainly of wool and cloth—Britain's staple product in Roman times and one that was to dominate our trade until the seventeenth century—but slaves, taken from the north and west, turn up with some frequency and at the time of the Norman Conquest the port of Bristol was involved in this activity as it was to be once again in the eighteenth century.

Internal long-distance trade was minimal—land travel was

73

more difficult and expensive than seafaring and perhaps as dangerous, for Athelstan's *Laws* contain the regulation "if a stranger leave the road and neither shout nor blow a horn, he is to be assumed to be a highwayman". Necessary products that were only found in certain areas included iron (Gloucestershire, Sussex, Northamptonshire, Lincolnshire and Yorkshire); lead (Derbyshire and Somerset), and salt (Sussex, Dorset, Droitwich, Cheshire), and these of course had to be moved across country.

Most trade, though, took the form of the short-distance exchange of local manufactures and agricultural products. The upkeep of bridges was essential to these movements and by the tenth century it was meticulously organized. At Rochester bridge, for example, "the second pier is the responsibility of Gillingham and Chatham, including planks for five and a half yards and three beams".

It was in the country that almost everyone lived and on the fields that everyone certainly depended. Unfortunately very little is known about the structure of the village and, though excavations have been undertaken at about fifty sites, there is nothing for the traveller to see. Meanwhile the experts are themselves fiercely divided over the interpretation of their work. The whole question is complicated by the fact that most Saxon villages have remained in occupation ever since and all trace of the original settlement has in consequence disappeared. The village sites that have survived and can be examined are therefore not typical; they are the failures, or they would not have remained untouched. Here what has been found usually takes the form of small huts with sunken floors and, more rarely, larger rectangular barn-like halls.

The structure of country life was the same in Saxon and Norman England. The land was usually farmed on a two-field or three-field system of rotation—barley, wheat and fallow. The emphasis was thus on grain; the word 'lord' is derived from 'keeper of the bread', 'lady' from 'kneader of the bread' and the lord's men are his 'loaf-eaters'. The evidence suggests that barley was by far the commonest crop, the very word 'barn' meant the 'barley place'. The other main crops were rye (the Saxons knew August as 'rye-month'), oats and wheat. St Cuthbert tried to grow wheat on the Farne Islands but found it would not do,

74

turning to barley he was much more successful. From barley too was brewed the ale which was the universal Saxon drink. Sheep and pigs were the commonest animals, the principal sources of milk and cheese were ewes and goats—cows were much rarer. Oxen were employed as draught animals, horses were not much used for agricultural work and were very expensive. Tenth-century records provide a scale of values: horse, 120 pence; ox, thirty; cow, twenty; pig, ten; sheep, five pence.

A large estate might produce a very varied list of products. The eighth-century laws of King Ine of Wessex give as the food-rent from 1,000 acres; ten vats of honey, 300 loaves, forty-two containers of ale, two cows, ten geese, twenty hens, ten cheeses, one container of butter, five salmon, twenty pounds of fodder and 100 eels.

Agricultural implements included the plough, harrow, scythe, sickle, bill-hook, spade and pitchfork. Something of these can be seen in manuscript illustrations in the British Museum and a little in various folk museums; the most remarkable survival is perhaps part of a tenth-century plough with a moveable mould-board, now in the Castle Museum at Norwich. Farm-carts were of the type still common today in southern Europe, having sides of loose staves or wattle which could be fitted or removed as required. The only source of mechanical power was the water-mill. The earliest known example is recorded in Kent in 762 and by the end of the Saxon period there were 5,600 mentioned in the areas covered by Domesday Book. There were also a few mills worked by animal power, but the wind-mill had not yet reached the west.

The plough ruled all. A contemporary proverb ran "man to the plough and the spear, woman to the spindle". Every agricultural calculation referred, directly or indirectly, to the ox-drawn plough. Thus the acre was a furrow-long (furlong) by a pole (five and a half yards, the distance required to turn the plough) and its area represented, at least in theory, a day's work. Records often deal in a much larger unit, the hide, but this was not a standard measurement, it was a unit of assessment, comparable with money of account or rateable value.

Society was in detail complex, particularly when the Saxon structure was overlaid by a Danish pattern, but in essence it was a two-tier affair of thegns and churls. The thegn, a landed noble-man, held his property by title-deed and owed the king three services; military duty, the construction of fortifications, and the repair of bridges. There were considerable variations of actual status. A thegn might be a royal retainer, or a man who would in later centuries have been called the lord of the manor, or a knight.

Whatever his position, there was a great gulf fixed between the thegn and the churl. The word meant literally 'a husband-man' and the churl might be defined, loosely, as a free peasant not bound to the soil, but owing services to the lord in return for the land he held. As time went on there was an increasing tendency to replace food-rents by labour-services and there is no doubt that the general drift was from unqualified freedom to a more servile condition. The fundamental line of cleavage between thegn and churl was normally impassable. One contemporary declared firmly that even if a churl prospered to such an extent that he had a gold-plated sword, the noble weapon, yet "he is nevertheless a churl". There is also a statement that "if a churl prospered, owned five hides, a church and a kitchen, a fortified gate-house and a special place in the king's hall—then he is entitled to the rights of a thegn". This sounds like irony. Beneath the churl there was a class of slave labourers—a group so obscure that it is impossible to estimate their numbers, but one which is regularly mentioned in laws and regula-tions.

Whatever the differences in status, there was little in the style of clothing, variations showed themselves rather in the quality of the cloth and of the accessories—jewellery and arms. The cloth itself was normally homespun and decorated with braid made by tablet-weaving. Men wore combinations and over these cross-gartered trousers or tights together with a three-quarter length belted tunic and, when required, a cloak. Women's dress consisted of the kirtle, an all-concealing over-garment, and a head covering. Personal toilet offered them opportunities for display—as early as the seventh century there occur complaints that nuns were curling their hair and trimming their nails to a point, like the talons of a hawk.

Weapons were for men almost a necessary form of dress.

Although the greater part of most lives was peaceful, warfare and danger formed part of the background of society. Of all weapons the sword, that status-symbol, was the most prized, the most useful and the most powerful. It was a two-edged instrument, thin and straight, about thirty inches long and housed in a wooden scabbard which often was lined with fleece, for the lanolin in the wool kept the blade from rusting. A sword and its sheath could be worth as much as seventeen slaves. In the ninth century a rather different type made its appearance, perhaps introduced by the Vikings; it was heavier, stronger and with a more efficient hilt.

In general use was the all-purpose scramasax, a single-edged knife anything from fourteen to thirty inches long used in daily life as well as in battle. A throwing axe, a sort of tomahawk, was occasionally employed in warfare, while by the time of the Conquest the housecarles of the royal bodyguard carried a formidable two-handed axe. Bows and arrows are known to have been used, but hardly anything tangible has survived.

The commonest of arms were the spear and the shield. The spear, like the scramasax, was in everyday use; spearheads are the most widely distributed of all weapons and in pagan times were placed in the graves of men of all classes. The ashen shaft was about six feet long, the head anything up to two feet. Shields varied from twelve to twenty-eight inches in diameter. The early ones were very light, being not more than half an inch thick. In later centuries they became heavier and convex with a central boss protecting the grip. This boss and the rim were of iron, but the shield itself was still made of wood and an example has been found in which thin layers of lime-wood were arranged with the grain of each layer running at right angles to its neighbours as in modern plywood.

The ordinary fighting-man relied on leather for protection. Only two metal helmets have been found, the one at Sutton Hoo and one at Benty Grange in Derbyshire. This latter was a sort of crash helmet with a nose piece and although only the iron framework has survived intact it is clear that this was filled with plates of horn riveted to the iron. It is now in the Sheffield City Museum at Weston Park. Examples of the commoner weapons can be seen in many local museums, but the most comprehensive collection is that in the Early Medieval section of the British Museum.

Methods of fighting were not sophisticated. On 11th August 991 Saxons and Danes met near Maldon in Essex and the poem describing this encounter gives some indication of how such matters were carried on. The Saxons ride to the battle field and then dismount and, leaving their horses behind, form a wall of shields. Having done this, they advance. The two bodies of men fire arrows, throw javelins and finally engage in hand-to-hand contests, using first spears and then swords, in the course of which the shields are hacked to pieces. One gets the impression of a very slow, very personal struggle. At Maldon it is the Saxons who lose the day, but they stand and fight even after defeat is certain and on the death of their leader—a huge ealdorman whose body was examined at Ely in 1769 and found to measure six feet nine inches—one of his followers shouts—

> Mind must be firmer, heart stronger, courage greater,
> As our might lessens.

IV

SAXON ENGLAND
924—1066

1 *The Great Days: 924–975*

Maldon took place during a second period of Scandinavian
pressure. Before it was fought there had been fifty years of
triumph for the house of Wessex. Edward the Elder had been
succeeded by his son Athelstan (924–939) who rounded off the
English kingdom. In the north he conquered the Norse state of
York in 927 and on 12th June in that year he held court at
Eamont Bridge on his new northern boundary, at which the
kings of Scotland and Strathclyde and the English lord of Bamburgh swore to support him and to suppress idolatry within their
lands. The site was probably the prehistoric 'henge' monument
of Mayburgh, 360 feet in diameter, with an entrance on the
east, a high bank of turf-covered stones and a single stone nine
feet high at its centre, which stands just south of Penrith to
the north of A592 (NY/523284).

Four years later Athelstan conquered the Celtic land of Cornwall at the other end of his kingdom and then in 934 turned
north again to invade Scotland, harrying the country by land
to Kincardinshire and by sea as far north as Caithness. It was
during this campaign that he presented to the shrine of St Cuthbert the vestments already described in Chapter II.

These victories brought into existence a coalition of all those
who felt themselves threatened and in 937 the king was opposed
by a combination of Norsemen and of men from Scotland and
Strathclyde. There was a fierce battle at Brunnanburgh, perhaps
Bromborough on the Wirral peninsula, in which the English
were victorious though their losses were heavy.

Athelstan was a many-sided man, a great general but also a
collector of works of art and of relics, a law-declarer, a "lord

of warriors, a ring-giver" as a poet described him. His own coins proclaim him "king of all Britain" and he was a figure of international importance, in touch with the rulers of Scandinavia, the Emperor and the Normans. On his death there followed three short reigns and then came the apogee of Saxon rule, the rule of his nephew Edgar (959–975), a strong, capable man whose reign was a time of peace sandwiched between times of warfare.

In May 973, having already reigned for fourteen years, Edgar was crowned on Whit Sunday at Bath by the great St Dunstan. The king was then aged thirty, the canonical age for becoming a priest, and the coronation service with its theological-political overtones was a national anthem to success in both fields—and one that has continued almost unchanged in form to the present day. Modern historians consider as 'well-founded' the story that as a sort of post-coronation celebration Edgar was rowed on the river Dee by seven or eight subject kings, though one feels that this may have involved no more than a symbolic dipping of the oars—compare the modern laying of a foundation-stone—rather than anything very energetic.

By this time England south of the Humber–Mersey line had been divided into shires which, apart from the later creation of Rutland, remained virtually unchanged until 1974. In the south and east the boundaries followed the traditional Saxon areas and eastern Mercia was shired along the lines of the Danish settlements, but western Mercia was divided into new artificial units, shires named after a central town and of a standard size —artificial creations like the French departments set up at the time of the Revolution.

Viking destruction had shattered monastic life in the north and east. No new church building can be attributed with any certainty to the second half of the ninth century, between 887 and 956 there is a significant gap in the recorded succession of bishops, ancient sees such as Lindsey disappeared for good and the country as a whole was without organized monastic life. Peace now gave the opportunity, while a man and a movement provided the impulse, for the revival of the English church.

Not only here but throughout northern Europe monasticism had fallen on evil days. Then in 910 a reformed movement began at Cluny in Burgundy and spread rapidly. The scope of the Cluniac reforms was both theological and administrative. There was a return to the strict rule of St Benedict and all Cluniac houses were united in a single international body, subject to the authority of the mother house. In this way the abbot of Cluny eventually became the master of no fewer than 1,450 dependent units in each of which discipline and routine were identical.

The man who brought these reforms to England was St Dunstan. Born about 910 the son of a Somerset thegn, he became abbot of Glastonbury in 940, was temporarily exiled in the 'fifties and at Ghent came into contact with the new movement. He was recalled by Edgar and consecrated Archbishop of Canterbury. From that time until his death in 998 he worked at the reconstruction of the church in England. In the Bodleian there is a manuscript of Ovid, made at Glastonbury about 960, which includes a drawing of Dunstan at Christ's feet, said to have been done by the saint himself. Dunstan owed much to his disciples Oswald of Worcester and Ethelwold of Winchester. The latter in particular was a man of parts: he had a reputation as an architect and himself worked as a labourer at Abingdon until a falling piece of timber broke his ribs. On another occasion, when the canons of Winchester refused to become Cluniac monks he turned them all out.

The new men preached in Saxon. Alfred had tried to create a clergy educated in Latin, a laity educated in Saxon. He did not altogether succeed. The laity remained illiterate, while Latin became something of a mandarin language so that, a century after Alfred's death, Aelfric of Cerne Abbas, producing a Latin grammar, appears to have regarded it as being only for ritual purposes, while the living language was West Saxon. New Saxon place-names enshrined in charters, the work of clerics, suggest that this was so. *Buckland*, which exists in more than a score of modern places, means 'bookland', land held by charter; *Charlton* equally widely distributed, is 'churltown', indicating a subsidiary settlement on an estate—in Danish-occupied areas it becomes *Carlton*.

The Cluniacs dominated the revived church. In the eleventh century three-quarters of the bishops were monks, as were all

F

the archbishops until 1052, while at the close of that century the monasteries held about a sixth of the landed wealth—Glastonbury, Dunstan's starting point, being the richest. The consequence was a great age of church building and rebuilding and it is from the years between 950 and 1066 that four-fifths of the existing Saxon churches date. Nevertheless it was a consequence confined to southern England. In 1066 there was still only one monastery in the shires of Lincoln, Leicester, Nottingham, Derby and Yorkshire, while twenty years later there were still no monasteries in Northumbria.

What remains does not necessarily give a true picture of the distribution or the size of typical Saxon churches. On the contrary, the pattern has been affected by the presence of good building materials. Most of the churches are, significantly, on the limestone ridge that runs from Yorkshire to Dorset or on the chalk uplands from Norfolk to Salisbury Plain. Churches built of wood certainly existed and some stone churches had timber bell-towers, but only one wooden church still stands. This is at Greensted (TL/539030) in the former forest lands of Essex on the minor road west from Ongar, nineteen miles north-east of London on A128. The walls are built in Scandinavian style of oak logs, split and pegged together and set in an oak base. (The wood itself is not necessarily tenth century—it is said that nothing remains of even such a recent structure as Nelson's *Victory*, the timber having all been replaced over the years.) It was at Greensted that the body of St Edmund rested in 1031 on its way to Bury St Edmunds.

There were seventeen cathedrals; some, including Canterbury, York, London, Winchester, Leicester and Rochester were on Roman sites which had regained their old importance, but many were in small places of no significance, for a Saxon cathedral was not intended to be a large building.

When the Normans came they were shocked by these unimpressive boxes and pulled them down as quickly as possible, but by great good luck the foundations of one small Saxon cathedral can be seen at North Elmham (TF/988216) in Norfolk. At East Dereham, midway along the Norwich–Swaffham road (A47) turn north on B1110. The cathedral lies just beyond the parish church of North Elmham. A church stood here from the end of the seventh century until 1072 when the see was moved, first to Thetford and then to Norwich. In 870 the early building was destroyed by the Danes, who were probably responsible for raising the earthwork that can be seen round the church (the mound in one corner though, is likely to be Norman). After the defeat of the Danes the church was rebuilt in the tenth century.

What now survive are the foundations of a western tower and staircase and an aisleless nave all of which probably pre-date the Danish destruction. The eastern end, consisting of a transept with two minute towers and an apse, represents the tenth-century rebuilding. The whole thing is tiny, only 123 feet long, and has the especial charm that attaches to the minuscule together with the practical advantage that the whole plan can be taken in at one glance.

Next in importance to the cathedrals, at least in the early days, were the minsters, or mother churches, each responsible for a considerable area. They were run by groups of clerics, part of the bishop's staff, not monks but secular clergy living a col-legiate life similar to that of the cathedral community in which they had been trained. In their heyday there were about 250 of these minsters and from them the clergy went out to the sur-rounding settlements where there was usually still no church but only the consecrated enclosure or 'preaching field'. Gradually local churches were built which became the centre of individual parishes, the area being withdrawn from that served by the minster, and the parish priest lived in the community, farming a little land and perhaps married—though some declared forth-rightly "a priest's wife is the devil's snare".

Early monasteries had been established in Roman forts at Bradwell, Burgh and Holyhead, but their organization was full of local eccentricities and it was largely due to St Wilfrid that these were replaced by the conventional Benedictine rule, or *regula*—hence the term 'regular' clergy. By the early eleventh century there were thirty monasteries and half a dozen nunneries and by the Conquest the number had risen to about fifty, many founded as offshoots from the great southern abbeys at Abingdon, Ramsey and Glastonbury. Hardly anything can be seen of these today, but a good deal of work has been done at Glastonbury and it is considered that by the mid tenth century it was comparable with the largest monasteries on the Continent. There were glassworks and at least eight smithies in operation.

In general, it is the small, out-of-the-way Saxon church that still stands. The general style of late Saxon architecture changed little from that described earlier, but some new features do appear which help one to identify later work. The basic ground plan was that of a rectangular nave with a small square or rectangular chancel to the east and a square tower to the west, and one of the features of tenth- and eleventh-century churches is the strength of these towers. Solidity was particularly necessary because of the new practice of bell-ringing which reached England from the Continent at about this time and their strength has helped the towers to survive when the remainder of the church has been rebuilt. An attractive feature are the pairs of narrow round-headed belfry openings separated by a thick shaft set back from the outside surface of the wall. In the churches already described at Brixworth, Corbridge and Monkwearmouth, the towers were added or improved at this time. There is an attractive tower at the west end of St Benet's, Cambridge, with these typical narrow belfry openings. Strong defensive towers include those at Clapham (TL/035525, A6 just north of Bedford) and at Wickham (SU/394715, north of A4 between Newbury and Hungerford) where—significantly—there is an entrance eight feet above ground level. At Sompting, on the outskirts of Worthing, there is the only tower which still has its original roof, here a Rhineland pattern like a sharpened pencil.

The most easily recognizable of the detailed features to look for in these later churches is the existence of long-and-short work, those dressed stones alternately set vertically and horizontally. Walls are often decorated with blind arcading or stripwork, the latter consisting of slightly raised patterns that seem to imitate scaffolding and were perhaps derived from the timber work of wooden churches. The doorways and the windows though wider than in earlier centuries are still comparatively narrow, usually round-arched but sometimes having triangular heads—this is always a sign of late work. The windows are often double-splayed inwards and outwards, the object being to let in the maximum of light and the minimum of wind and rain, as windows were hardly ever glazed. Oiled linen was sometimes fitted, but normally the only protection was that of wooden shutters pierced by a few holes. In one or two churches—Barnack, for instance—there is evidence that the windows were blocked with slabs of pierced stone.

Any selection must be something of a personal one, but the following are, for one reason or another, particularly interesting:

Barnack, Peterborough: (TF/079050, B1443 three miles south-east of Stamford); C1/C3, windows, lower part of tower, pilaster-stripwork, seated Christ.

Barton-upon-Humber (Lincs): (TA/035219, A1077 fourteen miles east of Scunthorpe); C1/C3, forebuilding, and tower seventy feet high which is the body of the church, stripwork and blind arcading, triangular-headed doorway.

Boarhunt (Hants): (SU/604083, A32 north from Fareham, fork right almost immediately); C , chancel arch and walls.

Bosham (Sussex): (SU/804039, south of A27 Chichester–Portsmouth); C3, tower, chancel arch and greater part of the fabric. On the Bayeaux Tapestry Harold is shown sailing from Bosham.

Bradford-on-Avon (Wilts): (*see* Chapter II, p. 57).

Breamore (Hants): (SU/153189, west of A338 Christchurch–Salisbury and eight miles south of the latter); C1, stripwork, mutilated rood in south porch *c*. 1040. See especially the south transept arch with its Saxon inscription "here the Word is revealed to you".

Dover (Kent): C1, above the Castle. Surrounded by oval earth-work, possibly strengthened in 1066; door from western gallery of nave into Roman lighthouse.

Earl's Barton (Northants): (SP/852638, east of A45, Northampton–Wellingborough); C1, tower sixty feet high, perhaps once the body of the church; the best late exterior in England, with triangular-headed doors and windows, long-and-short work, and over all blind arcading and strip work.

Great Paxton (Hunts): (TL/210641, on B1043, Huntingdon–St Neots); C3, a very wide chancel arch, and an aisled nave, uncommon.

Repton (Derbyshire): *see* Chapter II, p. 58.

Sompting (Sussex): (TQ/161056, eastern outskirts of Worthing, two miles north-east on minor road); C3, original tower roof; interior, tower arch, frieze panels (*c*. 1000).

Stow (Lincs): (SK/882820 west of A15, ten miles north-west of

Lincoln); C, transepts (1006–1016); the Norman work is even finer, especially the chancel, west doorway and font.

Wing (Bucks): *see* Chapter II, p. 59).

Worth (Sussex): (TQ/302362, south-east outskirts of Crawley, about two miles off B2036), C3, unusual windows in nave, impressive apse, chancel arch said to be the largest Saxon one (twenty-two feet high).

Often the most interesting work is a piece of carving, perhaps easily overlooked, in a church which may have no other Saxon features. Many of these are considerable works of art. They were not always recognized as such. Less than fifty years ago the leading authority on the period went out of his way to describe them as "rustic art" which was "ill-informed and worse-executed". Today the pendulum has swung and art historians see the work of Saxon artists as superior to that of the Normans. Indeed the Saxon influence persisted for at least a century after the Conquest.

At Winterbourne Steepleton (SY/629898, B3519 off A35 Dorchester–Bridport) there are superb flying angels similar to those already mentioned at Bradford-on-Avon, Breamore and Deerhurst. Roods, in various stages of mutilation, are fairly rare. The most lovely is the uncommon draped figure at Romsey, off A3057 north-west of Southampton. At Headbourne Worthy (SU/487319, west of A33 and one and a half miles north of Winchester) there is an unusual rood showing not only Christ but also St John and the Hand of God. Other roods include one at Daglingworth (SO/993049, west of A417 a few miles north of Cirencester), two at Langford (SP/248025, east of A361 Swindon–Burford) and one at St Dunstans in Stepney.

Figures include one of the Virgin, dated about 1060, at Inglesham (SU/205984, on A361 a few miles south of Langford) and a superb sculpture, probably eleventh century, of the Virgin and Child in York Minster, very strongly Byzantine in feeling. Different in every respect but equally remarkable is the angular carving of the Harrowing of Hell dating from the first half of the eleventh century and now in Bristol Cathedral.

Sundials were probably common, but only a couple of dozen dating from this period can now be seen. The number of divisions varies, but six is the most general. Usually they are scratched in the stonework and easily missed, but at North Stoke (SU/610865, twelve miles north of Reading and just west of B4009 from Goring) there are signs of carved hands holding the dial, as there also are at Langford. Quite the most interesting dial is in the North Riding of Yorkshire at Kirkdale (SE/677857, north of A170 between Helmsley and Kirkbymoorside). It is above the south porch and is framed by the inscription: "Orm, son of Gamal, bought St Gregory's church when it was all broken and fallen down and he had it made new from the foundations for Christ and St Gregory in the days of King Edward and of Earl Tosti". Tosti is Tostig, King Harold's brother, and the dial was carved when he was Earl of Northumbria (1055–66). Above the dial are the words "This is the day's sun-marking at every hour". The dial itself is divided into ninety-minute sections from 6.00 a.m. to 6.00 p.m. with a special mark for 'daytime' at 7.30 a.m. Below the dial is carved "And Hawarth made me and Brand, priest".

These names are Scandinavian—evidence of an influence that, especially in the north, produced a more highly complicated form of ornamentation than that of the Saxons. The most typical and exciting shapes are those of the 'Great Beast'—strange stylized ribbon-shaped animals that tend ever increasingly towards abstract patterning. There are good examples, perhaps as early as the mid-ninth century, to be seen on grave slabs at Plumbland in Cumbria (NY/150385, west of A595 Cockermouth–Carlisle and east of B5301 towards Aspatria) and at Levisham in the North Riding (SE/848910, west of A169, Pickering–Whitby), but the most dramatic is the slab from St Paul's Churchyard. This superbly calligraphic animal, originally painted in three colours, its body decorated with white spots like a Victorian rocking-horse, is believed to be a memorial to one of Cnut's ministers, Toki.

Scandinavian gravestones are often of the easily recognizable 'hogback' shape—long ridged stones with a convex profile, thought by some to represent a house of the dead. They can be seen in many places in the north—easily accessible examples are those around the Giant's Grave in Penrith churchyard. Sometimes the ends are supported by bears, though it often takes the eye of faith to make these out today. There are good bears, dating from the late tenth century, at Brompton in the North Riding (SE/374964, just beyond Northallerton on A684), where there are also three crosses.

Crosses dating from this period are not uncommon in the north and west, some of Scandinavian design but many that are cultural hybrids. The finest, not to be missed, is that at Gosforth in Cumbria (NY/073036, east of A595 about twelve miles south of Whitehaven), a cross that will stand comparison with the great Bewcastle and Ruthwell crosses. Its slim tenth-century shaft is fifteen feet high: on the east face is Christ crucified above two soldiers, one of them holding a lance; on the north face a man on horseback; on the west another mounted figure and two men fighting, and on the south face a number of animals. A mile or two east of Gosforth there is a good cross in the church-yard at Irton (NY/092005).

Crosses of particular interest include ones at Whalley in Lancashire, Darley Dale in Derbyshire and in the nave of St Peter's church at Leeds. At Halton in Lancashire (SD/499647, north of junction 34 on M6 and A683 from Lancaster) there is an eleventh-century cross combining carvings of the Crucifixion and the Resurrection with others from the pagan age of Sigurd, including one of his horse Grim. Among crosses in central and southern England one might notice those at Stapleford (SK/488373, on B5010 from Derby towards Nottingham) with a human figure and a rather earlier one with beasts in the collegiate church of St Peter at Wolverhampton. In Devon there is a good cross, well-placed, at Colyton (SY/246940, south of A35 Axminster–Honiton).

Many later crosses have wheel-shaped heads—a pattern imported from Ireland. They are very common in the west, with over 400 examples in Wales and a large number in Cornwall. A nice one is that at Whitford in Flintshire a mile or so north of the church (SJ/29788), its Welsh name Y Maen Achwyfan meaning 'the stone of weeping'.

Stone work is durable, wood is not. It is surprising, therefore that one, and perhaps two church-doors can still be seen. At Stillingfleet in the East Riding (SE/599410, eight miles south of York on B1222) the strapwork of the iron door hinges is fashioned into Viking ships and dragon heads and should not be missed. Nor should similar work at Stapelhurst in Kent (TQ/790350, nine miles south of Maidstone on A229) depicting a sea monster.

Minor works of art include two silver chalices only five inches high, one at Hexham and one found at Trewhiddle in Cornwall and now in the British Museum. Associated with the latter there was a small silver scourge of plaited silver, a ritual rather than a practical object. A large number of little ivories have been preserved. Especially attractive are two in the Victoria and Albert Museum, a five-inch crucifix dating from the middle of the tenth century and the head of a crozier about the same size but made a hundred years later, while in the provinces there are in the City Museum at Winchester angels swinging censers and at Liverpool a Nativity with a very pensive St Joseph, beautiful objects no more than three inches high.

2   The End of the Saxon State: 975–1066

Not, precisely, the end of Saxon England for that survived until at least the middle of the next century in a Saxo-Norman culture of which the Saxon element became increasingly diluted as time went by.

During the period 975–1066 the Saxon culture already described reached its peak, yet at the same time the state which had made that culture possible was suffering a series of disasters. King Edgar had died at the early age of thirty-two, leaving behind him two young boys, Edward and Ethelred, the sons of different women. Edward, thirteen-years-old, became king. His mother had been betrothed but never married to his father and he himself is described by Professor Stenton as a youth of "intolerable violence in speech and behaviour". It was a situation of which the thegns, resentful of the favour shown by the late king to the monastic reformers, might well profit.

Three years after his coronation Edward visited his brother Ethelred's mother—to whom their common father *had* been married—at Corfe. There was a scuffle in the courtyard and Edward dropped from his horse, dead. His body was buried obscurely in near-by Wareham and Ethelred became king. The episode was not only dramatic but also psychologically important. The murder of his half-brother hung, albatross-like, around

Ethelred's neck for the next thirty-eight years. Soon the Ealdorman of Mercia had dug up Edward's body and removed it to Shaftesbury where it was reburied in state—and almost at once miracles conveniently began to take place at the tomb of Edward 'the Martyr'. They did not stop and after thirty years Ethelred found it advisable to institute the festival of *Saint* Edward (March 18th).

It was very unfair; Ethelred was not more than thirteen at the time of the assassination, which had clearly been inspired by his unprincipled mother. But he was always an unlucky man. Machiavelli has written that to succeed a prince needs both a strong character and good luck. Ethelred had neither. Throughout his reign he behaved like a man unsure of himself, and he inherited a deteriorating situation. The regional ealdormen were beginning to flex their muscles, while as early as 965 Danish raiders had reappeared, establishing themselves at Scarborough. In 980 raiding began in earnest and there was to be continuous pressure for the next thirty years.

These raids did not lead to extensive settlement as the ones in earlier centuries had done. Their immediate objective was, one might say, financial and their ultimate victory was political. In 994 a 'treaty' was signed: there was to be perpetual peace in return for a payment to the Danes of 20,000 pounds of silver pennies, the most highly sought-after coinage in northern Europe. Eight years later the king paid another 24,000 pounds of 'Danegeld', while in 1008 the rate had risen to 30,000 pounds.

Ethelred did what he could. In 991 he ordered the setting-up of an army and a navy, and nine years later he himself led a successful expedition against the enemy at his backdoor, the Britons of Strathclyde. But contemporary comments in the *Chronicle* make it clear that there was no steady policy: "in the end it effected nothing but oppression of the people, waste of money and encouragement of the enemy"; "when the Vikings were in the east, the army was in the west"; "nothing went right in the south or in the north"; "anything counselled never stood for a month". Ethelred's own name meant 'noble counsel'; now men said he should have been called 'Unred' or 'no counsel', and today he is still Ethelred the Unready.

Matters moved to a crisis. In 1012 the Archbishop of Canterbury was murdered by the Danes, who this time took home 48,000 pounds. Next year Swein Forkbeard, King of Denmark, came himself. Disembarking at Gainsborough he was accepted as king in the lands of the old Danelaw and from there raided savagely into Wessex. Ethelred retired to Normandy. A bishop preached on the text 'the end approaches' and men sang the Saxon lament:

> Where is the horse?
> Where is the horseman, the giver of gifts?
> The walls are fallen, the halls are fallen,
> The lords are fallen.

Within three years both Swein and Ethelred were dead, and Swein's son Cnut (Canute) ruled over not only England but also for a time both Denmark and Norway.

It was in effect the end of the Saxon state, even if technically it survived for another fifty years. A Norse poet enthused that the new king "killed or drove away all Ethelred's sons, every one of them", though Cnut was careful to make it appear that nothing had changed. He sent to Normandy for Ethelred's widow Emma, married her and raised a family which had at least its share of Saxon royal blood. He replaced the 'ealdormen' by 'erls', but these were essentially the same type of royal deputy. The intermittent Danegeld was replaced by regular taxes, probably just as heavy, raised to pay for a standing army and a permanent navy.

Cnut was an international figure and for the first time since Roman days England was part of a continental empire. There was peace for all, prosperity for merchants and traders, the possibility of an interesting career for young noblemen, and "merry sungen the monkes in Ely".

This Danish interlude was brief. Cnut died in 1035, aged about forty, and by 1042 his sons Harold and Harthacnut were both dead—the latter was only twenty-five when he dropped "as he stood at his drink" at a wedding banquet. In the previous year he had invited Ethelred's son Edward back to England from Normandy and now, in the spring of 1043 Edward was crowned king. The blood of Alfred ran in his veins, but his mother Emma was a Norman and Edward himself, probably born in 1005, had been taken to Normandy when he was not much more than ten years old and had spent the next twenty-five years abroad. Now this middle-aged half-Norman became King of England. The Norman conquest had begun.

Historians find the character of Edward the Confessor something of an enigma. So did his contemporaries. In exile, says Professor Brooke, the king had been accustomed "to hunting and idleness, and these tastes stayed with him all his days. In later life he acquired a new hobby: . . . piety." He collected clergy from Lorraine, from France, from Normandy itself. He fathered no children and it was rumoured that his marriage was never consummated. That marriage had been to Edith, daughter of Earl Godwin of Wessex, one of the group set up by Cnut. Godwin was a stupid man who thought himself astute—a sometimes dangerous and always irritating combination. As a new man who had come to power by supporting Cnut and marrying into the latter's family he was unpopular among his peers. Now it appeared that Edward had come under the influence of Godwin and of his son Harold. Other Saxon families, of greater antiquity, fumed.

Perhaps Edward was not so easily influenced as men thought. He may have intended to stand above party, playing off Saxon, Norman and Scandinavian, one against another. In the early days Scandinavian influence seemed to be gaining a foothold, then, briefly, the Normans were in favour. Godwin was exiled, Duke William of Normandy was encouraged to believe that he was the king's chosen successor, a Norman became archbishop of Canterbury, Cnut's tax financing England's defences was abolished, and Edward's Saxon wife was removed from court. The king turned his attention to the building of an abbey at Westminster to be modelled on that of the Norman abbey at Jumièges, begun on Duke William's orders in 1040. It would seem that the Norman influence had triumphed in every possible field. Yet within a year the situation had been reversed. Godwin was back and the Normans were out—men said that they had "promoted injustice and counselled folly".

Matters were never quite the same. The house of Godwin, fearing another volte-face, dug themselves in and consequently became increasingly unpopular. Duke William continued to regard himself as Edward's chosen heir, or was at least careful to give the appearance of doing so. The uncanonical substitution of a Saxon for the Norman archbishop led to the new man's excommunication by three successive popes and, ultimately, to papal support for the Norman Conquest.

At Westminster, however, the work went on unchecked. Of Edward's abbey (1050–65) nothing remains today, but the *Vita Edwardi* mentions "a tower reaching up with many spiral staircases and, above these, walls rising to a wooden roof covered with lead" and the Bayeux Tapestry shows something of this. Jumièges, the prototype for Westminster, survives as an impressive ruin in a bend of the Seine south of N182, the secondary road from Le Havre to Rouen.

Meanwhile there were still Normans in England and some of them, men of moderate estate, had been given lands on the Welsh border. For two centuries relations between Wales and England had been good. The threat from Norse raiders had led the Welsh princes to associate themselves with the Saxon rulers of Wessex, but recently there had been renewed antagonism. The Norman settlers, encouraged to carve out estates for themselves, built fortifications which it is convenient to call 'castles', though they were no more than earthen ringworks consisting of a bank with a stockade and gate-tower, surrounding wooden buildings and a mound. The sites of three of these, controlling the valleys to the north and south of the Black Mountains, are known: at Hereford; at Ewyas Harold (SO/384287, reached by B4347 off A465, Abergavenny–Hereford) where, west of the church, there is a mound seventy feet high and a half-moon enclosure; and Richard's Castle (SO/483702, off B4361 five miles south of Ludlow) where the mound can also still be seen.

So far as is known there were no Saxon castles of even these primitive types, but a fortified house existed at Sulgrave in Northamptonshire, where the stone footings of a hall, a two-storey block and a free-standing tower dating from about 1020 have been examined, and there are signs of a similar tower at Portchester.

In 1053 Earl Godwin died and was succeeded by his son Harold. King Edward gradually withdrew from active political life. It was probably in 1064 that Harold was at Duke William's court in Normandy, helping him at the siege of Dinan, after which "William came to Bayeux where Harold took an oath to Duke William"—or so the Bayeux Tapestry asserts. Modern authorities are inclined to accept the statement, but wish they knew a little more about the terms of this oath. Unfortunately, as Professor Stenton comments, "a piece of stitchwork can only deal in superficialities".

King Edward died on 5th January 1066 just as men were putting the finishing touches to his abbey and, typically, left behind a muddle. A century later he was declared a saint—almost as odd a choice for canonization as his namesake Edward the Martyr, but the then king, Henry II, perhaps owed his throne to Edward's indecision, though he would have been the last to admit it. In 1066 blood claimants to the English throne included the king's young nephew Edgar; King Harold Hardrada of Norway, a descendant of Cnut; and Duke William, Edward's first cousin once removed. But hereditary succession was by no means yet the rule and it was Harold, who was pure English and on the spot, who "succeeded to the kingdom as the king granted it to him and as he was chosen thereto".

As soon as William heard the news he began to prepare for the invasion of England even though, says William of Poitiers, many Normans "thought the enterprise too difficult". The Duke was seven or eight years younger than Harold, expert and practised in modern warfare, having fought successful campaigns against the King of France and the Bretons, and having conquered Maine to the south of Normandy. He controlled, directly or indirectly, the ports that faced England from the Scheldt to Finisterre and he had the support of the Pope. However, he was short of men and so he spent the early part of the year building up a force which eventually consisted not only of his own tenants, but also of foreign mercenaries, some of them landless knights coming from as far away as southern Italy.

Meanwhile Harold's difficulties were increasing. King Hardrada of Norway was preparing to assert his claim to the throne. Tostig, Harold's brother, who had left England in 1065 after quarrelling with him, was lurking in Scotland. Almost equally worrying, in a different way, had been the fact that, according to Florence of Worcester, at the end of April a "hairy star was seen, not only in England, but—or so they say—throughout the entire world, shining for seven days with great brightness" —Halley's comet.

On 8th September Harold sent to their homes the local militia who had stood to arms throughout the summer, for now the harvest must be got in, and moved the fleet to the Thames estuary, while four days later William transferred his fleet from its station close by Caen to St Valéry near Abbeville on the Somme, a move commemorated there today in the names Port Guillaume and Harold Tower. The distance from the new base to the English coast was less than eighty miles, but north winds kept him in port. And now King Hardrada, helped by those same winds, sailed from Sognefiord north of Bergen to Tyneside where he was joined by Tostig. They ravaged the coast to the south and then sailed up the Humber to Riccall. On 20th September the Danish king drew up his army at Fulford. The Saxons were defeated in the ensuing battle and, York having surrendered, the invaders encamped close by at Stamford Bridge.

The news of the landing had reached Harold about 18th September. Moving with great speed, he had reached Tadcaster, nine miles from York, by the 24th and next day he was storming into the enemy camp. The fighting was fierce and decisive. Tostig and Harold Hardrada were both slain and a handful of ships was enough to take the survivors home. It was one of the most complete victories of the Middle Ages. Seventy years later heaps of bones yet marked the site and in the twentieth century the battle was still being commemorated by an annual local feast at which pears baked in boat-shaped pies called 'spear-pies' were eaten.

But meanwhile in the Channel the wind was now south-east. Stamford Bridge had been fought on a Monday; on the following Thursday William landed at Pevensey about nine in the morning. The battle near Hastings was fought less than three weeks after Stamford Bridge. In that short time Harold somehow managed to settle affairs in the north, to cover 190 miles back to London and then, hardly pausing, to continue for a further sixty miles to the south coast. It was a remarkable achievement, but it was also perhaps a mistake. William gave no sign of moving rapidly inland but seemed, wisely, determined to remain in touch with his ships. Harold's men were tired, his army of 6,000–7,000 was not more than half his potential force. Time was on his side. Perhaps, though it is not in character, Harold planned a holding operation. If so, he was disappointed. As soon as William heard that the English were approaching the coast he moved forward. He needed a quick victory.

On Saturday 14th October battle was joined. Harold had the better position, his men drawn up at the 'hoar apple tree' on what is now Caldbec Hill, a ridge running for about 600 yards, its flanks protected by a steep drop, though to the front the fall was much less—only about twenty yards from the crest to the little valley that lay between the Saxons and the Normans. The army was a mixed bag of peasant militia stiffened by the royal housecarles, trained men but old-fashioned in their tactics, accustomed to forming a shield-wall, fighting on foot and armed with their traditional two-handed battle-axe.

The Normans had moved from their landing beach at Pevensey, having put up some sort of fortification in the Roman fort there, to Hastings. Now they advanced by way of Telham Hill (460 feet high, crossed today by A2100) to face the enemy. William's army was probably slightly smaller though more powerful, for it consisted of handpicked professionals, expert and practised, and was strong in cavalry.

The first attack on the English position failed, but as the line went back in disorder the English broke from the shield-wall and, pursuing the enemy, were themselves cut off and suffered serious losses. Twice this pattern was repeated, perhaps deliberately so far as the Normans were concerned. The fighting continued all day until about five in the afternoon by which time Harold was dead and the battle had been lost and won.

The best account of the invasion and battle is not a written work but that unique survival, the stitchwork of the Bayeux 'tapestry'. This was probably commissioned by William's half-brother, Bishop Odo, for the opening of his new cathedral at Bayeux in 1077. It is likely that it was worked in England and, if so, in Kent. It consists of a number of pieces of linen about twenty inches wide totalling today just over 230 feet in length. The design was first drawn on the linen and followed in stem-stitch. The resulting outlines were filled with laidwork, parallel stitches held by threads at right angles, the latter being about an eighth of an inch apart.

Over forty per cent of the work deals with events before 1066 and only some twenty-five per cent with the battle itself. Beginning with Edward the Confessor on his throne, it is likely that it once concluded with William the Conqueror similarly enthroned, but there is a section missing from the end. It is surprising that matters are no worse, for the work has had a hard life. At the time of the French Revolution it was used to cover carts, while in the nineteenth century it was mounted on wooden rollers to be wound and unwound repeatedly as people viewed it. In 1803 Napoleon temporarily installed it in Paris as a prelude to the invasion of England. Goebbels is said to have had similar plans.

Miraculously, it has survived, packed with information— there are 626 figures and about 700 animals, beautifully worked in eight colours—about all manner of things; the building of ships and castles, the serving of food, methods of transport, styles of dress and so on. No written description is an adequate substitute for a sight of the thing itself, housed in a special gallery, well-designed if rather clinical, in the former Bishop's Palace beside the cathedral at Bayeux. Several English books contain reproductions of the whole tapestry; the definitive survey being *The Bayeux Tapestry*, edited by Sir Frank Stenton for the Phaidon Press in 1958. A smaller book, with the same title, is the King Penguin by Sir Eric Maclaglan, published in 1943.

An account of about 1070 says that Harold "fell covered with deadly wounds" and on the tapestry below the words *Rex interfectus est* (the king is killed) a Saxon is being hacked down by a Norman on horseback. The story that Harold was killed by an arrow in his eye probably arose from a confusion with a figure to the left of this group.

Harold's unconsecrated body was buried on the cliffs above the seashore and William began a careful, methodical advance by way of Romney to Dover and thence to Canterbury where he halted about four weeks. Then he moved to Southwark but, like the Romans before him, decided that a direct attack on

London would be too difficult. Instead he swung west, crossing the river at Wallingford and receiving the submission of English leaders at Berkhampstead. He moved on slowly over the last twenty-five miles to London, harrying the countryside as he went, to be crowned on Christmas Day in Edward the Confessor's new abbey, the service being in both French and English. He then rested outside London at Barking while a temporary keep was built on the site of the present Tower. The march had been marked by the construction of a number of such temporary keeps—the tapestry shows men with pick and shovel hard at work at Hastings—but nothing of these can be seen today, except possibly at Dover, where the bank and ditch to the south of the Saxon church may have been raised in 1066.

William ordered a tax to be levied on all men and the confiscation of the lands of those who "stood against me in battle and were slain there". These matters having been attended to, the Conqueror felt secure enough to return to Normandy in March 1067.

V

THE NORMAN CONQUEST
1066—1100

The Duchy of Normandy was the creation of Scandinavian raiders who had arrived there in the early tenth century, probably from the south by way of the Loire. They had created a sort of French Danelaw and, exhibiting their usual knack for survival and assimilation, by the time of the Conquest they were French in their speech and their culture, well-established in an area stretching along the Channel coast from Mont St Michel to a point east of Dieppe and extending about fifty miles inland —the southern boundary of the duchy being approximately on the line of the modern N12.

Duke William had been born at Falaise (about twenty miles south of Caen, on N158). The existing castle, in spite of what one may be told, is later in date, being early twelfth century. In its chapel there is a modern memorial carrying 315 names of those who came over with the Conqueror. The Duke was thirty-five years old at the time of the Conquest and had already been ruler of Normandy for twenty years. In appearance he was probably tall, stout, his hair already thinning; in character he was certainly a man slow to make up his mind but swift to act once he had done so, his originality the fruit of meditation not intuition. He had learnt his military lessons beating off the repeated attacks of the King of France, the last as recent as 1058. In the following year his marriage—significantly, to a descendant of Alfred—had finally been recognized by the Papacy, for it was within the prohibited degrees, in return for William's promise to build two religious houses. These, largely paid for out of English resources, are the Abbaye-aux-Hommes and the Abbaye-aux-Dames at Caen. They contain respectively the graves of

William and his queen and their style exercised an important influence on Norman building in England.

William returned to England at the close of 1067. As the land was parcelled out among his followers a succession of revolts occurred. He quelled an outbreak in the south-west with comparative ease and ordered the immediate construction of a castle at Exeter. Today the gatehouse probably dates from this time, being an odd mixture of Norman plan and Saxon detail, notably two triangular-headed windows and what looks suspiciously like long-and-short work.

There had also been rumblings in the north and there too William showed the flag, ordering the erection of castles at Warwick, Nottingham and York on his outward journey and at Lincoln, Huntingdon and Cambridge on his way south. It was not enough. Before the close of 1068 the King's representative in Newcastle had been killed and at Durham the Norman commander was burned to death in the bishop's palace. At much the same time a Danish force landed and seized York.

William acted with speed and decision. He drove off the Danes and punished the Saxons. Harrying the north in a deliberate manner he made a desert and called it peace. The Anglo-Norman chronicler Ordericus Vitalis records that William "gave orders that all corn, cattle, farm implements and food was to be collected in heaps and burnt, thus destroying everything that could support life north of the Humber". Twenty years later the area had not recovered and Domesday Book indicates that the counties of Cheshire, Shropshire, Staffordshire and Derbyshire were also affected.

The defeated Danes sailed south and put in again at the Wash. The local inhabitants, many of them of Danish descent, seized the Isle of Ely and were joined there by a Lincolnshire thegn, Hereward the Wake. From this base they carried on guerrilla warfare, sacking Peterborough where a Norman from Fécamp had recently been installed as abbot. William bought off the Danes and then turned his attention to the rebels. Communications with Ely ran by way of Aldreth, a point at which the Ouse could be crossed, and it was from here that William conducted his siege. Ely did not fall till 1071 when Hereward escaped and is said to have continued to resist for a time in the forests around his home at Bourne, north of Peterborough. The exact position of Aldreth is not known, but a possible candidate is Belsar's Hill at Willingham (TL/423703, on B1050 north of Cambridge).

The frontiers of his new kingdom must now be looked to. In 1072 William led an expedition into Scotland, whose King, Malcolm III, had shown himself only too ready to harbour refugees from England. The two men met at Abernethy on the south bank of the Firth of Tay and Malcolm paid homage to William. It was a gesture rather than a decision; the problems on that border were not to be solved so easily.

In Wales a forward policy was pursued with some temporary success, though the *Chronicle* over-simplified a little when it recorded simply that "Wales was under the king's rule and he built castles there". In 1081 William did indeed place a castle at Cardiff, but in general he relied on three new border earldoms —it is noteworthy that the only earls created by the Conqueror were men in charge of the frontiers of Wales, Scotland and the Channel—based on Chester, Shrewsbury and Hereford. From these centres it was hoped that the earls would extend Norman rule westwards.

The land had been terrorized into submission, the frontiers secured, it remained to see what was the new pattern of lordship and of wealth. As the Bayeux Tapestry gives an unmatched picture of the Conquest, so too Domesday Book provides a unique record of England at the time of that Conquest—a record that is also a jungle, not impenetrable, but one that has not yet yielded up all its secrets.

It was decided in 1085 to find out by enquiry from juries of local inhabitants the agricultural wealth of each place, both at that time and as it had been in 1066, to record what tax it paid at each of those dates, and to group this information under the names of landholders, the object being to construct a record of tenants-in-chief and of the value of their holdings. Towns are not described in much detail, castles and churches are almost ignored, there was no attempt to conduct a census of the population. Those were not subjects about which the king was interested in obtaining information. Conditions of land-holding and the structure of taxable wealth—these were what mattered.

Nevertheless, modern investigators have been able to extract by torture answers to some of the unasked questions: thus the record provides a figure of 283,242 heads of households, suggesting a population of not less than 1,375,000. Those interested in the local pattern of distribution will find brilliant analyses in the various volumes of *The Domesday Geography of England*, edited by H. C. Darby.

The Domesday Book—so nicknamed, as Richard fitzNigel put it, "because it spared no man but judged all men indifferently as the Lord in that great day will do"—was the product of a government enquiry unequalled for efficiency and comprehensiveness until the nineteenth century. Contemporaries were not always enthusiastic. The *Chronicle* comments "so exactly did he have the survey made that there was no land, not even—it is a shame to tell but it seemed to him no shame to do—an ox or a cow or a pig that was not set down". Today Domesday Book is in the Public Record Office in Chancery Lane. An accessible modern translation is in course of publication by Phillimore of Chichester.

It is unlikely that William, that tidy-minded man who so disliked loose ends, ever saw the final version of his enquiry, for in the summer of 1086 he left England never to return. In September of the following year he was injured during fighting at Mantes, forty miles north-west of Paris, and after lying ill for a time at Rouen he found that town too noisy and was moved to St Gervais where he died, aged about sixty. He lies in his Abbaye-aux-Hommes at Caen, his tombstone a comparatively modern one. A monk at the abbey wrote of him as being "large and strong . . . temperate . . . eloquent and easy to understand, though with rather a hoarse voice" and for a moment one thinks one is getting near the man. Unfortunately the description is lifted from one of Charles the Great—itself derived in its turn from some words of the Roman historian Suetonius! (Similarly, the very individual portrait of King Edward in the Bayeux Tapestry was copied from an illuminated manuscript depicting King David.)

The Conqueror left behind three sons and an ambivalent reputation. To the Normans he not unnaturally appeared a great ruler, firm and just; the *Anglo-Saxon Chronicle* equally naturally, records a different character:

> He was very wise and powerful, stronger than any of his pre-decessors, mild to good men who loved God, immeasurably stern to men who went against his will, a very stark man and terrible to those. Truly in his time men suffered great hardships—he ordered castles to be built, he took gold and silver from his subjects, he ordered that his men should blind any who poached deer, for he loved the tall deer as if he were their father. Rich and poor complained, but he was so very stubborn that he did not care. Alas that any man should be so proud! May God show mercy to his soul and forgive him his sins!

William's three sons were Robert, nicknamed Curthose (Shorty), who inherited the duchy of Normandy; William II, known as Rufus (Red Face), now aged about thirty, who ruled England until his sudden death in 1100; and Henry, the youngest, who succeeded Rufus in ambiguous circumstances, and reigned till 1135. A modern historian has commented, *tout court*: "the Norman rulers of England were disagreeable men, masterful, stern, cruel"—a description which can be extended to cover the half-Norman Angevins—Henry II, Richard I and John—who succeeded them. But these men were also in general successful and it is noticeable that the two comparatively civilized rulers, Robert Curthose and Stephen (1135–54), were also the failures. To succeed it was necessary to be unpleasant.

William Rufus, a man like his father in character and in general appearance, though rather shorter and with a noticeable stammer, has had a bad press. He tangled with the Church and it is the Church's assessments that are on record—in general the 'bad kings' in the Middle Ages turn out on closer inquiry to be those who gave trouble to that undying institution, the Christian Church. Of course William was difficult: he kept church appointments vacant and pocketed the income. "Are not the abbeys mine?" he retorted when protests were made; there was constant friction with the Archbishop of Canterbury, St Anselm—"God's face, I do what I like"; and the King had a pragmatical if very human approach to honesty. "Who", he asked engagingly, "can be expected to keep *all* his promises?"

This should not be allowed to obscure William's achievement

in strengthening the royal hold over England. A weak king could have undone all the work of the Conqueror and the country have broken up into rival feudal lordships engaged in endemic civil war—a situation that did occur, temporarily, half a century later during the reign of Stephen.

Immediately after his accession there was a rising in the west country which the King's firm action broke. In 1091 Rufus invaded Scotland and forced Malcolm—responsible in all for no fewer than five invasions of England—to renew his oath of obedience, for what that was worth. More to the point, the English King overran Cumbria, blocking the western route by a castle at Carlisle. Three years later he suppressed a rebellion in the north-east and took over the strategically valuable castles at Tynemouth and Bamburgh. Only the Welsh and the weather remained out of his control. Of the former the *Chronicle* noted that they "ever retired into mountains and hills so that it was impossible to come at them", while in the same year "there was very unseasonable weather; and as a result through all the country the crops turned out only middling".

In 1096 there occurred an event full of significance for the future. William's elder brother, Robert Curthose, pawned the Duchy of Normandy to him in exchange for a loan of 10,000 marks to enable Robert to go a-crusading—an unnecessary adventure typical of this affable, unpractical man. In 1100, Robert, now on his way back from the First Crusade, rested in Apulia and while there married Sybil, a daughter of one of the Italian Normans, in this way acquiring at one stroke a dowry sufficient to redeem Normandy and the possibility of an heir who might succeed to both the Duchy of Normandy and the Kingdom of England, thus disappointing the hopes of the youngest son, Henry.

In that same year William went hunting at Brockenhurst in the New Forest. The area had been afforested by his father in 1079 and comprised about 180 square miles—today it still covers something like 140—and was only one of a number of districts withdrawn for the King's use from the normal feudal land structure. Such areas were not necessarily wooded, but the New Forest was indeed a forest. The main quarry were the red stag, the fallow deer and the wild boar, hunted with the brach, a sort of foxhound that worked by scent, and the large alan or wolfhound.

The hunting party which set out on Thursday, 2nd August, included the Lord of Poix in Ponthieu, Walter Tyrel, and in the course of the day's hunting, according to William of Malmesbury, "Walter let fly an arrow which shaved the hair on the animal's back, sped on and wounded the king standing beyond". In fact he had killed the king. "A few peasants carried the body to Winchester on a wagon, blood dripping from it all the way", and there the king was buried. (When the cathedral tower collapsed shortly afterwards men said it was in protest at Rufus' wickedness, but the matter-of-fact William of Malmesbury thought that it was only because it was so badly built.)

Meanwhile the most extraordinary stories had begun to circulate—one is reminded of the death of President Kennedy—and have continued to do so ever since. They fall into three groups; accident, ritual murder and political assassination. It is not impossible that the King was hit by a ricochet, as suggested by Ordericus Vitalis, though he was writing some thirty years after the event. Ritual murder is an exciting but wildly improbable anthropological dream, nowadays completely discredited. It rested largely on the tradition that on that morning the king had said to Tyrel "Walter, do justice according to these things which you have heard", the implication being that it was his duty to sacrifice the royal victim.

But the King's words will bear a different interpretation—that he had confided to Tyrel information concerning a plot against the throne. The man who benefited from William's death was his brother Henry, a member of the hunting party and a sufficiently cold-blooded man. He rode straight from the forest to near-by Winchester, secured the royal treasure and then made for London where he was crowned only three days later at Westminster. It was all very smooth. Tyrel fled to his estates in France. He got nothing, but his wife's relations in England received high honours. And Henry—he had become King in the nick of time, for within a month Robert Curthose, Rufus' nominated heir, was back in Normandy. Finally, William's elder brother Richard had been killed accidentally while hunting. Like the throne, the idea had been there for the taking.

If William's death is shrouded in mystery, an almost equal uncertainty surrounds the very different question as to whether or not the Conquest, firmly established by 1100, was a 'good thing' for England. The Victorians had no doubt that it was, today we are not so sure. One thing is clear. The Norman success was complete, a tribute to efficiency, abounding self-confidence and speed. The Normans were not over-inventive, but they had a clear appreciation of priorities and would beaver away at a limited range of basic structures. Their success was so rapid and so permanent that it is tempting to believe that the Saxon state was inevitably doomed, unstable and even perhaps on the point of dissolution into independent earldoms. In fact the Old English kingdom possessed more advanced administrative machinery than did the Duchy of Normandy which was still a state in the making, its dukes not fully independent, its boundaries ill-defined. With England the Normans inherited a strong political machine, with unusually broadly-based revenues.

To the English aristocracy, of course, the Conquest was a disaster. Domesday Book records only two Englishmen among the 200 principal tenants-in-chief, while ten Normans held nearly a quarter of the wealth of England. Ordericus Vitalis makes no bones about the matter, "the natives", he says, "were crushed, imprisoned, dispossessed, scattered abroad".

The new ruling class was a racial minority and it maintained itself by what was, at least to begin with, a military occupation. Whether or not feudalism existed before 1066—and the point is still hotly debated—it certainly did so after that date. There was increased emphasis on the tenurial relationship between the tenants-in-chief and the King, and between these men and their tenants, the former being responsible for law and order within their lands and for the supply of over 4,000 knights.

The new order was characterized by the introduction of two contemporary, Continental, inter-locking features; the armoured horseman or knight, and the defensible post or castle, and it was the Normans who first linked them firmly together. One must not over-glamorize the knight. Originally the word signified no more than a retainer. The Norman knight has been described as "a person of small means and insignificant condition. His equipment was elementary, and his only title to distinction was his proficiency in mounted warfare" (Stenton). His castle was a wooden tower in a fortified enclosure and he himself was a hybrid, something between a formidable military machine and a rather unimportant tenant-farmer. One thing he certainly was not—a chivalrous knight-at-arms. The society in which he moved was, observes Professor Barlow, "a restless, drunken and emotional society, gorged after 1066 with unaccustomed wealth."

These men figure in the Bayeux Tapestry and also on other, less well known, objects. They stand in their armour around the Temple Pyx in the Glasgow Art Gallery; they battle again in the carvings of St George and the fight at Antioch over the church doors at Damerham in Hampshire, and in Dorset at Fordington on the outskirts of Dorchester. During the twelfth century their armour changed hardly at all. The sword remained the main offensive weapon and body-armour consisted of a long shield, a conical headpiece and the hauberk, a lengthy shirt of mail consisting of thousands of separately forged and riveted links. At the very close of the twelfth century the conical helmet was replaced by a sort of barrel covering the head, the shield became smaller and more triangular, the hauberk shortened to knee-length and was covered by a sleeveless linen surcoat. In this, as in so many other ways, the Norman age had come to an end.

The castle was a comparatively new type of fortification. In its simplest form, a two-storeyed tower, it appeared first in the area between the Loire and Normandy about the year 1,000. In England it now became the chief instrument used by king and tenants (technically on his behalf) to administer the new land. About three dozen were already in existence by 1070 and by 1086 the number approached a hundred. Their function was at least as much manorial as military. As a rule they were situated near roads, rivers and settlements—about half are attached to towns though, notably, they are often outside the town walls.

In general these early castles conformed to a standard pattern known as motte-and-bailey. The motte (nothing to do with a moat, but a French word meaning a clod of earth and hence a mound) was a large, flat-topped earthen mound, usually artificial and sometimes as much as fifty feet high and 100 feet in diameter at the top, in shape rather like a Christmas pudding.

This carried a timber tower and stood in an attached base-court, the bailey (enclosure), usually on the latter's circumference. The bailey was surrounded by an earthen bank, topped by a wooden stockade entered through a wooden gatehouse, and outside the bank was a V-shaped ditch the farther scarp of which was protected by a hedgehog (hérisson) of brambles or thornwork.

The smaller castle was a military base for a handful of soldiers, not a country house but a barracks, and the tower on the motte was in effect an elevated fighting platform. The bailey—all of it within a bowshot of the tower—contained the everyday wooden buildings: hall, well, kitchen, stables, store-rooms and huts for the men-at-arms. The whole was elementary but effective, rapid in construction and economic in technique and labour —though this was not a major consideration since 'castle-work', much resented, was one of the obligations of all tenants.

In towns a space was ruthlessly cleared to provide suitable sites. At Lincoln 166 houses were destroyed and Domesday Book provides plenty of other examples, while archaeologists have uncovered the foundations of Saxon huts lying below the castles at Oxford and Peterborough. The process of raising mottes continued until the middle of the twelfth century for, says the *Chronicle*, "they built castles far and wide throughout the land", so that today literally hundreds can still be seen. There are particularly heavy concentrations on either side of the Welsh border—in Montgomeryshire alone at least fifty mottes are known—and in the south-west of Wales.

Since their towers were built of wood it is hardly surprising that nothing remains, but the Bayeux Tapestry gives pictures of five castles of the motte-and-bailey type (Dol, Rennes, Dinan, Bayeux and Hastings) which agree in detail with the written descriptions, one of the clearest of which, in the *Life of John, Bishop of Thérouanne*, is that of the building of a castle in Flanders near Dixmude, early in the twelfth century; "in those parts nobles make an earthen mound as high as they can, and surround it with a ditch. Round the upper part of this mound they construct a strong wooden wall with as many towers as they can manage. Inside this they place the keep, which overlooks the whole structure. The only way in is by a bridge which goes from the far side of the ditch to the upper part of the mound". Contrary to the popular picture, a moat was never a feature of most castles, though the ditches must often have had some rainwater in them; at Dixmude when the bridge to the keep broke a procession fell into three feet of water.

The Bayeux Tapestry shows a layered pattern on the side of some mottes. This was once thought to be artistic licence, but it is now known that a good deal of care was everywhere taken in the construction of these mounds. Alternate layers of large and small chalk rubble have been found at Carisbrooke; at Hallaton in Leicestershire there were layers of peat and hazel as well as clay and stones; at York a platform of oak slabs $5\frac{1}{2}$ inches thick resting on forked uprights consisting of roughly dressed trees about eight inches in diameter and over eight inches long was constructed, and in many places the mound was given a facing of clay.

Nevertheless the artificial motte was an unstable structure which would take ten years or more to settle sufficiently to support any form of stone building. In fact at most places it was a long time before the wooden tower was replaced by a stone keep and when this did take place the keep was often built not on the rather restricted area of the motte but somewhere else in the bailey, usually on its circumference. Castles were rebuilt as the need arose, or when a favourable opportunity presented itself, but in general the transition from the motte-and-bailey to the rectangular stone keep that sometimes stands today did not take place until the second half of the twelfth century (1154–1216). However there were, as always, old-fashioned builders and new-fashioned ones and it is normally very good going if a building can be dated within twenty years.

The highest motte is that at Thetford (A11, Newmarket–Norwich) which still stands eighty feet high within an Iron Age fort, though the castle itself was destroyed in 1174. Two other fine mottes now bare of buildings are in Essex at Ongar (A128, Brentwood–Harlow) and Pleshey (west of A130 a few miles north of Chelmsford). At Berkhamstead (A41) in Hertfordshire there is a good motte forty feet high though the surrounding constructions have been quarried to death. At York the two fine mottes raised in 1068–9 still stand, though the stonework is later, and there are interesting double mottes at Lincoln and

Lewes. The list could be extended indefinitely for mottes occur in almost every part of England, Wales and southern Scotland.

In most places the oldest stonework that is likely to have survived from the eleventh century will be a curtain-wall—so called because it 'hung' between small towers—built to surround the bailey. There are particularly interesting early examples at Brough in Cumbria (NY/790140, A66 east of Penrith); Peveril in Derbyshire (SK/148826, at Castleton on A625, Whaley Bridge–Sheffield), and at Ludlow in Shropshire. The finest example, however, is at Richmond in the North Riding on A6108, just south-west of Scotch Corner. The splendid keep is mainly of later date but almost all the curtain-wall on the north-east and north-west sides of the triangular site is eleventh-century work as are the lower parts of the four towers between which it is hung. The foundations of the wall were found to rest on a raft of holly and birch piles.

The best of the towers is the Robin Hood Tower, the first on the left of the present gateway, with two barrel-vaulted storeys and good arcading in the lower, St Nicholas' Chapel. In the south-east corner, adjoining one end of the early wall, is Scolland's Hall, one of the very few surviving eleventh-century castle halls. It was originally a two-storey building, the lower floor being used for stores while the upper floor was reached by an external stair through the fine archway that can still be seen. This floor was lit by two-light windows which have a rather 'Saxon' look.

The remains of two other early halls are on the Welsh border. At Chepstow in Monmouthshire the sandstone blocks of the original half of William Fitz Osbern, built by 1071, still stand with thirteenth-century work above them. Here again there were two storeys and the entrance at the east end has survived. The second hall, similar but less complete, is at Monmouth itself.

The chapel of Durham Castle, now the basement of later work, is about the same date, with six pillars supporting good eleventh-century capitals, excitingly primitive with their moustached faces, angular animals and straining supporters.

Larger centres required something more than a wooden tower or even a stone-built hall—something that could be used as a centre of government and a relatively secure residence. These needs could be satisfied by the erection of a stone keep, essentially a vertical stack of rooms: the basement held stores and often a well; over this was the entrance floor, usually reached for reasons of safety by way of an outside staircase and a small guard-room, and consisting of a public hall and perhaps one other room; above this was a floor of private apartments some of which were set into the walls themselves, bedrooms, cupboards, latrines and perhaps a small chapel or oratory. The cupboards were known as garderobes (wardrobes) and, with that misplaced delicacy which still persists, the word came to be applied also to the latrines. Today these can be distinguished from the other cavities by the fact that they include, for obvious reasons, some sort of shaft to the outside world. Above all was a high-pitched roof—usually levelled in later times for defensive purposes. The keep was known as the lord's *dominium* or lordship, corrupted to 'donjon' and then to 'dungeon', a name originally applied to the whole building.

Something of the arrangements in a small early keep can be inferred from a contemporary account of how the castle at Amboise was taken in the late eleventh century. Three men hid themselves in the basement. From there at night they climbed ropes by way of a sewer into a bedchamber on the next floor where they found the lady of the castle, two maids and a watchman—all asleep. One man drew his sword and held these captive while the other two men went up a ladder and through a trap-door to the roof where they raised the banner of their lord.

The walls of stone keeps normally consisted of a core of rubble faced with dressed stone, often cut in cubes about one foot square. If Roman bricks were available they were re-used, as at Colchester, and many castles in south-east England, where good building stone was scarce, include limestone brought over from Caen, for water transport was cheap, road haulage by contrast being slow, difficult and very expensive. For the same reason the best stone from castles has often been taken in later times, leaving the rough core exposed. This can be seen very clearly at Middleham in the North Riding where the original ashlar facing survives above the height to which robbers could easily reach.

There is not much evidence regarding the cost of building a castle in England in the eleventh or twelfth centuries, but figures relating to the building of Richard I's Château Gaillard (take D1 from Les Andelys) at the close of the period show that the cost of construction was made up as follows: raw material twenty-five per cent; transport twenty-five per cent; building fifty per cent. Wages comprised two-fifths of this last item, as stated in the Exchequer Roll, being paid to "hodmen with baskets, bags, hand-barrows and tubs, carriers of water in barrels, and watchmen".

It seems that in the erection of church towers and castle keeps an average growth in height of about ten feet per season was normal, operations being usually suspended from Michaelmas to Easter though, when the matter was urgent, work continued as long as possible and even night shifts working by candle-light have been recorded. The work was in charge of what was in effect an architect, though he is termed an artificer (*artifex*) or engineer (*ingeniator*).

Something of the rewards for top men can be guessed from the appearance in Domesday Book of land-holdings by "Stephen the carpenter", "Waldin the engineer" and "Radbell the artificer". Under these were the craftsmen, stone masons and carpenters, miners and excavators, makers of shuttering (*hurdatores*) and lime-workers. Towards the end of the twelfth century William Fitz-Stephen described the din when repairs were being effected at the White Tower "with so many smiths, carpenters and other hands working so vehemently with bustle and noise that a man could hardly hear the one next to him speak".

When a keep was finished the outside was plastered and white-washed, a fact to remember when looking at the rather forbidding exteriors today. The White Tower was once really white, and there is perhaps an added significance in "Child Roland to the *dark* tower came".

Most of the stone keeps in England were not constructed until about a hundred years after the Conquest, and from the years between 1066 and 1100 there are only two great stone-built keeps still standing, but these are two of the largest and finest in the country, the White Tower of London and Colchester Castle.

The Tower of London is so well known that it is necessary to pause for a moment, strip it of its later history and forget the guides who skim over its structural history as quickly as possible in order to get on to the history of its prisoners. For they came later. At first there was only the White Tower which, very little altered externally, stands today much as it was in William the Conqueror's reign, built then to serve as a royal fortress-palace. It was the largest buiding in Britain since Roman times, its plan a rectangle 107 feet by 118 feet, its walls of Kentish rag and Caen ashlar 15 feet thick at the base, placed close to the Thames in the south-east angle of the old Roman walls.

The supervisor and perhaps the architect of the work was Gundulf, Bishop of Rochester. He had visited the Holy Land and he may there have seen the Byzantine keep at Saône (Sayhun) and carried back in his head the general pattern which took shape in the Tower, for he was an enterprising man—in 1102 he supervised the opening of Edward the Confessor's tomb and on that occasion he was only just prevented by the Abbot of Westminster from pulling out a hair from the king's beard.

This picker-up of trifles also had the reputation of being "very efficient and expert at building in stone". Indeed so efficient was he that the Tower was probably finished within about ten years, though work on the surrounding area was still going on in 1097 when the *Chronicle* complained that "many shires which owe works to London were greatly oppressed in making the wall round the Tower".

The completed building consisted of a basement with three storeys above. The entrance (today a window) was at first floor level in the south-west angle or by a round stair turret in the north-east angle. Below the entrance floor was the basement, divided by a cross-wall which is carried up to the third storey. The second floor contains the chapel of St John in the south-east angle, 60 feet by 35 feet—exceptionally large for a castle—and very fine—Romanesque architecture at its most austere. The third storey of the Tower has within its walls a passage surrounding the entire structure, probably originally intended as a sentry-walk.

The stone keep at Colchester is the largest in England, its

ground plan measuring 152 feet by 111 feet, and though its upper storeys were destroyed in 1683 it remains an enormously imposing building. It was built near the centre of the town, not a usual Norman practice, but one adopted here for the very good reasons that its foundations are the vaulted base of the Roman temple once dedicated to the divine Emperor Claudius. It was too good a site for the Normans, those arch-improvisers, to disregard; the situation and perhaps to some extent the size of the keep were determined by this architectural bonus. Roman stones and tiles were also incorporated in the walls themselves, together with the ubiquitous Caen stone.

The decision to build here a keep rivalling even that in London may have been taken to protect the northern approaches to the Thames and also East Anglia itself, which Domesday Book indicates as being the richest part of England, against the Danes who had raided the area as recently as 1071.

The keep was built in the 'eighties and the design so closely resembles that of "the great tower" of London that it is thought the same directing intelligence was at work here, that of Gundulf of Rochester. The original entrance was on the first floor, and led to the great chamber which was divided in two by a cross-wall and provided with a chapel, in the south-east corner, comparatively large but less impressive than that at the White Tower. The other three angles are strengthened by buttresses. The fine doorway, which leads directly into the basement was put in a little later, in the time of Henry I. Today the castle contains the important Colchester and Essex Museum.

Apart from one or two very much smaller towers and sections of wall dating from the close of the eleventh century—as at Oxford, Pevensey and Corfe—there is little more to be seen of the first generation of Norman castles, but in ecclesiastical architecture the picture is very different. For one thing, everywhere the churchmen built in stone, so the chances of survival were much greater, and for another, the clergy despised what they had inherited. Just as the Saxon thegns were quickly replaced by Norman tenants-in-chief, so too the English clerics were replaced by Normans and by 1090 there was only one Saxon bishop left, St Wulfstan of Worcester. The names of Saxon saints were whenever possible struck from the calendar,

while the Abbot of Abingdon gratuitously referred to St Ethelwold as "an English peasant" and the Abbot of St Albans called
his Saxon predecessors "uncultured idiots".

Holding such views it is not surprising that the new men
began a great rebuilding. The Norman clergy wanted churches
of a Continental pattern, built in the manner known today as
Romanesque. Saxon churches like Saxon saints were, they felt,
peasant style. These old-fashioned stone boxes must be replaced
by something more suitable, more civilized, and even St Wulfstan was impelled by the new fashion to rebuild Worcester
Cathedral. Analyzing perceptively his own motives he wrote:
"we wretches destroy the works of our predecessors to get praise
for ourselves, for those happy holy men did not know how to
build stately churches". A generation later the Norman William
of Malmesbury had no such qualms: "churches rise in every
village, town and city; monasteries are built in a new style. You
do not know which to wonder at more, the beauty or the speed."

This great rebuilding produced the most highly developed
form of northern Romanesque architecture, one which carried
its features even further than in such Norman prototypes as
Bernay (N138 south-west of Rouen), the crypt at Bayeux,
Jumièges and Caen.

On both sides of the Channel the prime characteristic of the
new style was that the downward thrust of the building's
weight was concentrated at selected points instead of being distributed over the whole surface of the wall. One consequence
was that windows and doorways could be wider than in Saxon
work while another was that the remaining wall had to be con-
siderably thicker. Externally the thrust was carried by heavy
semi-circular arches over doorways and windows, while internally
it was brought to ground level by equally massive piers and
columns often eighteen feet or more in circumference and
usually fairly squat though occasionally, as at Tewkesbury,
rising to a height of as much as thirty feet. The great arches
were made to appear less heavy by the use of concentric arcs
of geometrical patterning—the most easily recognizable feature
of Norman architecture—but this work was always functional,
never merely decorative.

In addition to these structural features the larger Norman

churches are characterized by the great length of the nave and by a massive central tower. Largeness had been a feature in Normandy, but England outbid the Continent with such structures as the 86 foot internal height of Ely and the 554 foot length at Winchester, one of the longest in all Europe. In constructing these heavy central towers the builders frequently over-reached themselves and the towers later collapsed. A quite undeserved reputation for architectural expertise can be acquired by asking of any large Norman church "When was the tower rebuilt?" and it is no surprise that a thirteenth-century petition sometimes used at Evensong ran "And, deare Lord, support our roof this night, that it may in no wyse fall upon us and styfle us, Amen".

The great weight required strong foundations. At Durham these are fourteen feet deep, but sometimes the work was—quite uncharacteristically—scamped by the Normans. At St Albans it goes down only six inches and at Winchester too it is virtually non-existent. As in castle architecture so also in churches the walls consisted of a stone casing and a rubble filling —what Wren called "small rubbish-stone". In the hundred years during which the Romanesque style was fashionable in England this stone facing became increasingly sophisticated. Herring-bone patterns of rough stones or Roman tiles disappeared and there was a growing use of hammer and chisel rather than the axe for dressing stone, while quite early in the twelfth century thick joints in the masonry gave place to much thinner ones. William of Malmesbury wrote enthusiastically of the buildings put up by Roger of Salisbury, "the courses of stone are so correctly laid that the joint deceives the eye and leads it to imagine that the whole wall is composed of a single block".

At the same time the mouldings became more complex, their outline changing from one with slight curves and shallow cutting to a deeply cut pattern with strongly marked convex and concave faces. The Norman mason was originally not much of a carver and in eleventh-century buildings there is an almost complete lack of applied ornament, but in the next century decoration becomes increasingly elaborate and effective. Columns and piers are incised with geometrical patterns, blind arcading breaks up the walls, and the arches over doors and windows are worked with repeating designs, chevrons, rosettes and beakheads appearing in roughly that chronological order.

Naturally this architecture is seen at its most impressive in the cathedrals and the largest churches. An ideal Norman cathedral would have an imposing west front with two towers, while there would be a third at the crossing of nave and transepts (Southwell alone still possesses all three). Between the west front and the central tower the nave would be exceptionally long and both it and the transepts would carry three layers of arches; those dividing the nave from the aisles, above them the arcades of a gallery built into the thickness of the wall, the triforium, and over all the clerestory with arched windows looking out above the roofs of the aisles. Beyond the transepts there would be a comparatively short choir and beyond that an apse with a processional way, the ambulatory, that leads from the transepts round behind the altar and along which today tourists conscientiously tramp. The choir itself was the private chapel of monks and clergy and as such was to some extent an isolated unit which could be cut off from the rest of the church—a practice carried to its logical conclusion in Spain where the choir stands as an isolated stone box, impervious alike to worshippers and sightseers.

Though the church was perhaps planned from west to east, construction usually started at the east end and once the choir was completed the church was functional. It might be finished in less than thirty years or work might, as at Ely, drag on for a century so that before its completion the very style itself had changed.

The most important architectural event of the years immediately after the Conquest was the rebuilding of the choir of the Benedictine cathedral priory of Canterbury, work that was completed in ten years and of which William of Malmesbury wrote that "there was nothing like it in England for the light of its glass windows, the gleam from its marble pavements, and the coloured paintings that led fascinated eyes to the panelled ceiling". Today this is gone, burned down in 1174, after which the cathedral was rebuilt in the latest style, no longer Romanesque but Gothic—an event which conveniently marks the end of Norman church architecture.

Gervase of Canterbury's description of the later work throws light on building methods and dangers. "William of Sens procured stone from overseas, constructing ingenious machines for loading and unloading ships and hauling cement and stone. He made templates for shaping the stones". Later "he raised the arches and vaults. And having completed both sides of the triforium and clerestory he was at the beginning of the fifth year in the act of preparing machines for the main vaulting when suddenly the beams broke under his feet and he fell to the ground, together with stones and timber, a distance of about fifty feet". He was not killed, but he was unable to continue the work and retired, a permanent invalid, to Normandy.

What remains of the old Romanesque cathedral is the magnificent western crypt, 190 feet in length and the largest in any English medieval church, with splendid carved capitals showing animals playing musical instruments, lions and birds, fabulous monsters and jugglers—all themes apparently taken from the illuminated manuscripts of the Canterbury school. Since later builders found it unnecessary to reconstruct what were in effect the foundations of a church, Norman crypts sometimes survive rebuilding. During the twelfth century they became unfashionable and that at York was one of the last to be constructed. The recent excavations here should not be missed.

There are also Romanesque remains in the monastic buildings attached to the cathedral. Quite the most interesting are the eleventh-century arcading in the east walk of the infirmary cloister—by far the earliest in England—and the guest hall by the Court Gate with its Norman staircase.

Of the larger churches raised during the first generation after the Conquest there are two outstanding examples. The Benedictine abbey of St Albans (today the cathedral) has the earliest and best central tower. Inside, the north wall of the nave and both the transepts survive untouched. The style is massive and plain, and a good deal of Roman brick was used to make an attractive abstract pattern round the arches of the transept and crossing. There are also some Saxon balusters placed, interestingly but less successfully, in the triforium of the transepts. The nave is immensely long—521 feet and only rivalled in England by that at Winchester. The abbey was the work of a master mason named Robert. "He excelled all the masons of his time" says the Abbey chronicler, and he was paid with land at Sarratt worth sixty shillings, which he gave back to the abbey on his deathbed.

Blyth Priory in Nottinghamshire, reached by A634 between East Retford and Maltby, is today the parish church—all that remains of the Benedictine priory. What has survived, however, is one of the most complete early Norman buildings and stands in a most beautiful setting. The work in the comparatively short nave is even more austere than that at St Albans and has hardly been altered through the centuries.

The Norman work at the Benedictine cathedral-priory at Winchester is equally early, but much less complete. What can be seen is the fine crypt, the transepts and the entrance to the chapter-house. The great nave, built of limestone from the Isle of Wight, is also early but is now encased in later work, though a section of the original stonework can be seen in the eleventh bay on the north side. The central tower was rebuilt about 1120.

Above the choir are a number of large chests. In the twelfth century the bones of Alfred's father Ethelwulf together with those of other Saxon and Danish rulers were collected and put in these mortuary chests which were placed in the choir in the sixteenth century. In December 1642, in the first months of the Civil War, a troop of Parliamentary dragoons under the command of Sir William Waller toppled down the chests and scattered the bones all over the pavement. At the Restoration the chests were piously restored, but the bones of Saxon Ethelwulf are now inextricably mixed with those of, among others, the Danish Cnut.

The greatest of all the English Romanesque cathedrals is the Benedictine cathedral-priory of Durham. It has no rival in setting, unity of construction and architectural importance. It stands high above the city, like a fortress of the prince-bishops, its west front towering over the gorge of the Wear and best seen from the far side of the river—a magnificent work of art, very different from the "little church of stakes and branches" in which St Cuthbert's body had been laid a century earlier. The cathedral was built relatively quickly between about 1096 and 1125. The structure is all Romanesque apart from the east end beyond the choir, which is Early English, the central tower (1474), and the upper stages of the pair of western towers, added in the thirtenth century.

The nave consists of eight bays. Compound pillars alternate with cylindrical columns, the former carrying most of the weight, a neat solution to the problem of combining strength with variety, the columns themselves being decorated with deep-cut geometrical patterns. From the technical point of view the originality of Durham lies in the vaulting of the nave and choir aisles for here, a hundred years before it was used in any other English cathedral, is the ribbed vaulting which ultimately developed into Gothic. In southern Europe this type of vaulting, which had its origins in the east, had already been used in Lombardy, but the work at Durham is the earliest surviving example in north-west Europe, pre-dating anything in France by fifteen years or more.

From Durham masons went to work at Selby (1097–1123), fourteen miles south of York. Selby Abbey is a lovely church with an especially beautiful fourteenth-century chancel, but the work of the Durham men in the nave and the north transept can hold its own. Their work has also been identified as far north as Kirkwall in the Orkneys and as far south as Waltham Abbey in Essex.

The final stage of the Romanesque work at Durham was the erection of the rectangular Lady Chapel or Galilee. Work on a lady chapel was begun in the second half of the twelfth century in the conventional place at the east end of the cathedral but it was hampered by cracks—popularly supposed to be due to St Cuthbert's distaste for anything feminine so close to his bones! Eventually the chapel was instead built at the west end, an unusual position. It is a forest of slim pillars and decorated arches reminiscent, on a miniature scale, of the great mosque at Cordoba—it is almost unbelievable that it narrowly escaped being pulled down in the nineteenth century.

In this chapel is the tomb of Bede, on the outside of the north-west door of the cathedral is the large bronze sanctuary knocker in the shape of a dragon-head—for, as the Rules of Durham say, there were "certain men that did lie always in two chambers over the church door . . . that when any offenders did come and knock, straight way they were let in at any hour of the night". Close to the cathedral stands the former monastic dormitory, built in the fourteenth century and now the museum containing the Cuthbert relics.

Most other cathedrals in existence in Norman times still contain some Romanesque work and it seems simplest to list these in a geographical order, beginning in the north and moving in an approximately anti-clockwise direction around England. Except where otherwise indicated they were all Benedictine foundations. At Carlisle the Augustinian priory (1092–1120) —it became a cathedral in 1133—was begun after the city had been recovered from the Scots by William Rufus. It is a very odd building, for during the Civil War the nave was pulled down with the exception of its two eastern bays, and the stonework used to build guard-houses, so that today there is a very early, very short nave which, together with the west wall of the transept is the only Norman stonework left. Instead of piers running up to the roof there are very squat cylindrical columns supporting the nave arcade while above these the triforium and the clerestory are organized as separate levels. The emphasis is thus horizontal rather than vertical and gives a powerful fortress-like impression which is entirely suitable to a Border church.

A similar pattern of levels can be seen at Hereford (1079–1145) and at Southwell in Nottinghamshire (1108–1150). At Hereford there is imposing work in the choir, part of the south transept and the arcade of the nave. The remainder of the cathedral was destroyed by a great fire in 1786 after which the upper part of the nave was disastrously 'restored' by Wyatt so that today it is best, in order to appreciate the massive chunky columns and chevron mouldings, to keep one's eyes severely lowered so as to cut out the work above.

Southwell—which started life as a collegiate church of secular canons and only became a cathedral in 1884—is one of the best examples of Romanesque. More than half the original church still stands, comprising the west front, the nave, the transepts and the towers. The seven bays of the nave carry in its most extreme form the emphasis on horizontality already noticed at Carlisle and Hereford, the columns being only 9 feet high but 15 feet in circumference. Above the nave arcade there is a complete break, emphasized by a continuous string-course, and above this the heavy arches of the triforium echo those of the nave below.

Southwell is unique in still possessing its full complement of three towers. The two on the west front were recapped after a fire in 1711 but the new work is scrupulously in keeping—which is more than can be said for the perpendicular west window. The north porch, built about 1130, has a good inner doorway and arcading but is most noteworthy for another unusual feature, the existence of an upper room for the sacrist—the man responsible for the church fittings—which was furnished with a fireplace and built-in cupboards. Other interesting details include the early carvings on the capitals high up at the crossing, decorated with scenes from the New Testament. These are too often overlooked, partly because one really needs field glasses to appreciate them, and partly because of the more famous capitals in the chapter-house, carved in the next century. Finally, in the north transept there is an eleventh-century tympanum with an energetic carving of David and the lion together with St Michael and the dragon.

A cathedral that is something of a hybrid of the vertical and horizontal treatments is Gloucester (1089–1160), an abbey raised to the rank of a cathedral in Henry VIII's reign. It is unusual in having in effect three levels—the crypt, the normal ground level, and galleries in the triforium so wide that they could be used for worship. The crypt, completed about 1100, is large and contains some exciting primitive capitals, including heads with fierce moustaches. The nave has seven bays with pillars rising to a height of 30 feet. Then the vertical impression is broken by a string-course and comparatively small arches at the triforium level. The north aisle of the nave is Norman, but the south aisle and choir were remodelled in the fourteenth century as were the superb cloisters—the best in England—which are connected with the north transept by an unusually well preserved Norman passage-way (slype).

Not far from Gloucester is Tewkesbury Abbey, very similar in style and built about the same time, being consecrated in 1123. It is the finest non-cathedral church of this early period and certainly one of the largest, as big as some cathedrals. The nave has similar colossal pillars to those at Gloucester. The most impressive feature, though, is the west front (1130–40) with its dramatic round-headed arch, 60 feet high and 30 feet wide, the impact of which has been only slightly weakened by the insertion of a later window.

At the cathedral-priory of Worcester the remains of Wulfstan's rebuilding can be seen in the crypt (1084), the chapter house (1130) and the two western bays of the nave (1170). The crypt is large and beautifully simple with plain cushion capitals, while the chapter-house is not only the oldest surviving example of its type but also one of the biggest. Internally it is a circular room with a diameter of 56 feet, its roof (revaulted about 1400) supported by a central column, while externally it is a ten-sided structure. These polygonal chapter-houses were a peculiarly English feature, but no others were put up for another hundred years, the next being that at Lincoln built about 1220.

During the civil wars of Stephen's reign Worcester provided shelter for the townsfolk and later still, in 1216 Henry II's son John was buried here.

At Bristol the cathedral, at this time an Augustinian abbey, has a rectangular chapter-house, dating from the second half of the twelfth century, its walls decorated with an all-over pattern of arcading, which is very satisfying. There is blind arcading too on the upper courses of the twin Norman towers at Exeter. Built about 1120 they were originally outside the body of the cathedral, but were later incorporated as transepts, most unusual.

On the south coast the cathedral-college of secular canons at Chichester (1091–1148)—incidentally the only pre-Reformation cathedral visible from the sea—was erected when the bishopric was transferred there from Selsey. The south tower of the west front is original, the northern is a late nineteenth-century copy. Inside, the square piers of the nave and choir were at first no more than huge rectangular blocks of stonework, but in 1186 there was a serious fire and in the rebuilding the piers were cased with Purbeck marble shafts which have modified the effect. Nevertheless Chichester still conveys an impression of archaic austerity.

That impression is reinforced by its most remarkable feature, two stone panels each about three feet in height, showing Christ with Martha and Mary, and the raising of Lazarus. They were discovered in 1829, built into the eastern piers of the crossing and are now in the wall of the south aisle of the choir. The reliefs are of Purbeck stone, each made up of six courses of stones of varying sizes. Controversy still rages as to their date, their purpose and inspiration, their origin. Were they brought here from Selsey when the old cathedral was abandoned? Are they eleventh or twelfth century? What exactly was their function? What is not in debate is that they are one of the outstanding pieces of English medieval sculpture, not to be missed.

The most likely answers are that the work dates from about 1140 (in which case it was designed for Chichester not Selsey) and that it served as part of a stone screen at the western end of the choir. In the first panel the great striding figure of Christ is in the centre, facing Martha and Mary and flanked to the right by four apostles. The second panel is the more dramatic. Lazarus rises just left of centre while beyond him are the sorrowing figures of Martha and Mary. Christ, right of centre, is even more imposing than in the first panel, the face expressing concentration and pity. (The eye-sockets were once filled with coloured paste or glass.) The total impression is hieratic, there is something of the formal mask and wig about the expressions and the hair, and the sculptor's interpretation may have come from the mystery plays that were just beginning to be performed in churches.

At Rochester there is Romanesque work of various dates. The oldest structure, 'Gundulf's Tower', stands outside the modern building and consists of the ruins of a detached Norman belfry, the only remaining portion of the original Norman church built about 1080 by that Bishop of Rochester who was also responsible for the first castle here and for the White Tower of London. The nave and a part of the north side of the choir show Norman work of the mid-twelfth century with its typical round-headed arches decorated with chevrons. The west front dates from the same period, though the central window is fifteenth century and the whole front was restored in the nineteenth century.

Especially attractive is the doorway in this front, built late in the period (1166–70), its tympanum showing Christ in

Majesty flanked by the four Evangelists, and with elongated shaft figures reminiscent of Chartres, representing Solomon and the Queen of Sheba. The head of the queen is missing, a consequence of the same attitude of mind which led the Parliamentary soldiery to wreck the interior fittings, when they "so far profaned this place as to make use of it in the quality of a tippling place, as well as dug several saw-pits, and the city joiners made frames for houses in it".

Eastern England has three Romanesque cathedrals with particularly fine naves; Norwich, Peterborough and Ely. Norwich was established when the see was moved from Thetford in 1094, the cathedral being built between that date and 1145; practically the whole work has survived with very little change internally, so that Norwich is, next to Durham, the best-preserved of all Norman cathedrals. The pattern was to a large extent based on that of Fécamp from which town the first bishop, Herbert de Losinga, had come. A careerist who had bought his way into the hierarchy, Losinga declared, "I entered office unworthily, but helped by God's grace I shall leave it honourably"—a sentiment that was at least theologically impeccable.

Certainly the yellow stone of Norwich was a good memorial to leave behind. There is a powerful central tower, one of the few early ones that did *not* collapse, the spire of which was added in the fifteenth century to replace an earlier wooden structure. The nave is 253 feet long and 83 feet high with fourteen bays, the piers rising to its full height. The cylindrical pier of the ninth bay from the east marks the original west end, beyond which the nave was extended after a fire in 1175. The aisles have early vaulting like that at Durham, but the nave vaulting is fifteenth-century. There is a very magnificent clerestory stage with arches as high as those of the nave arcade backed by superb galleries between the inner and outer walls, from ground level best seen in the transepts.

At Peterborough the abbey was not raised to the status of a cathedral until the reign of Henry VIII. In 1116 an abbey servant is reported to have said to a fire that would not light "the devil kindle thee", upon which the devil obliged to such effect that the Saxon church was completely destroyed. In consequence Peterborough is a perfect example of later Norman work, choir, transepts and nave being built between 1118 and 1175. (The dramatic west front is a little later, Gothic not Romanesque.) There is an unbroken view down the nave, very high and very long, to the semi-circular apse beyond—a perfect picture of a Norman interior. The most remarkable feature at Peterborough is the wooden boarded ceiling of the nave which is the original twelfth-century timber roof, the only one to have survived. Although it has been repainted at various dates the decoration follows the original diaper pattern with figures. Off the south transept is the Prior's Doorway with good decoration dating from the second half of the century.

Ely became a cathedral in 1109, work having begun about 1080 and continuing intermittently until the close of the twelfth century. The nave and transepts were completed about 1130 and are in the simple undecorated eleventh-century style, the nave being 86 feet high, fractionally higher than in any other surviving Norman cathedral. The painted wooden ceiling here is not old. The later Romanesque work is at the west end where the front and the right-hand tower were completed about 1174–97. There was once a matching tower on the left but this has vanished completely and somewhat mysteriously, and the porch is later in date. Nevertheless, the surviving work composes well and is unlike that of any other cathedral. The arcading of the lower stages is pure Romanesque, but the higher stages have a slightly different, sharper appearance. Romanesque was evolving into Gothic even as the builders worked.

On the south side the Prior's Doorway is one of the gems of twelfth-century sculpture, made about 1140, its carving still sharp and almost unweathered today. Over the doorway is Christ in Majesty supported by two beautifully stylized angels. On either side of the door the outer moulding is patterned with roundels containing little figures and animals, while the next is decorated with scrolls inhabited by long-necked winged dragons, much more medieval in character than those that lived in Scandinavian work.

At Lincoln, a cathedral of secular canons, the west front is Romanesque. The great cavernous arches date from the eleventh century and the doorways themselves from the middle of the twelfth century, as do the portions of frieze at the northern and southern ends. This was originally arranged in rectangular stone panels as a continuous strip across the whole western front. The south showed scenes from the Old Testament, the centre depicted Christ in Majesty flanked by two apostles, the north was given over to the Last Judgement. Part of this central section is now in the cloisters, and some of the remaining panels have been re-arranged, but it is easy to recognize the grimly dramatic scenes in hell.

Finaly, two late Norman cathedrals are those at St David's, Pembrokeshire, and Oxford. The former, a far western outpost of Norman England, although not built till 1180 has a nave in the old-fashioned Romanesque pattern, but the little pointed windows in the triforium, a pointed arch in the most western of the six bays, and the carved leaves of the capitals all look forward to a new style.

The Augustinian priory at Oxford (1158–80), was created a cathedral by Henry VIII. The nave is low, only forty-four feet in height, and its large cylindrical pillars have been treated in an almost classical style with arches carried up to enclose those of the triforium, perhaps partly in order to give an impression of greater height. The effect is original and sophisticated, but not entirely successful. This may be due to the fact that the three western bays were pulled down by Cardinal Wolsey—given the chance he would have destroyed the remainder as well in order to build for his college a chapel rivalling that at King's—but in any case Oxford indicates that Romanesque had become an academic, not a living, style and it was time it gave place to something else.

VI

THE HEIRS OF THE CONQUEST
1100—1154

While the walls of these cathedrals were rising throughout England the country was ruled by two very different men, the Conqueror's son Henry I (1100–1135), and Henry's favourite nephew Stephen (1135–1154).

Henry was a short thickset man with dark hair and an unattractive personality, greedy, cruel and profligate. By his father's will he had inherited no lands, these went to his brothers, but he had received 5,000 pounds of silver and as his father lay dying he, so it was reported, carefully checked the weight. Now, on the death of Rufus, he had acquired the throne of England in circumstances that were, to say the least, suspicious.

Six years later he defeated his remaining brother Robert Curthose at Tinchebrai and added Normandy to England. Robert was imprisoned for the rest of his life, first at Wareham and later at Cardiff where he learnt Welsh and composed a poem in that language which includes the appropriately prophetic line "Woe to him that is not old enough to die", for he lived in captivity almost thirty years and was eighty when he died in 1134. He is buried in Gloucester Cathedral, his effigy being at the east end beyond the choir stalls. With unconscious irony his sword is half-drawn.

On his accession Henry, unlike Rufus, had seen the value of coming to terms with the Church, while at the same time he outwitted or terrified—he was a very alarming man—his secular enemies. The consequence was a comparatively uneventful reign, the greater part of which he spent in Normandy. In England the situation appeared stable enough and, though it rested very much on his personal authority, there was no indication of the baronial reaction that would follow his death.

South doorway, Church of St Mary and St David, Kilpeck; *see* p. 165 *(National Monuments Record, Crown Copyright)*

West front, Castle Acre Priory; *see* p. 139 *(National Monuments Record, Crown Copyright)*

Tympanum, Church of St Mary Magdalene, Stretton Sugwas;
see p. 168 *(National Monuments Record, Crown Copyright)*

Capital from the crypt, Canterbury Cathedral; *see* p. 118
(National Monuments Record, Crown Copyright)

St John's Chapel, Tower of London, *see* p. 113 *(National Monuments Record, Crown Copyright)*

The Castle Motte, Thetford; *see* p. 109 *(Aerofilms Ltd)*

(Above left) Orford Castle; *see* pp. 162–3 (National Monuments Record, Cr
Copyright); (*above right*) Newcastle Castle; *see* pp. 157–8 (Philipson Studi
(*below left*) Conisbrough Castle; *see* pp. 162–3 (National Monuments Rec
Crown Copyright); (*below right*) Rochester Castle; *see* p. 134 (Nati
Monuments Record, Crown Copyright)

(Above) Rievaulx Abbey: the apsed building on the far side of the cloisters is the chapter-house; the range to its right is the dormitory and beyond that is the infirmary cloister. On the near side of the dormitory is the refectory; *see* pp. 144–9 *(Aerofilms Ltd)*.

(Below) East side of font, St Mary's Church, Luppitt; *see* p. 166 *(National Monuments Record, Crown Copyright)*

St Albans Cathedral, the nave looking east; *see* pp. 118–19 *(National Monuments Record, Crown Copyright)*

Durham Cathedral, the nave looking east; *see* pp. 119–20 *(Walter Scott)*

Rochester Cathedral, the nave looking east; *see* pp. 124–5 *(National Monuments Record, Crown Copyright)*

Southwell Cathedral, the nave looking east; *see* pp. 121–2 *(National Monuments Record, Crown Copyright)*

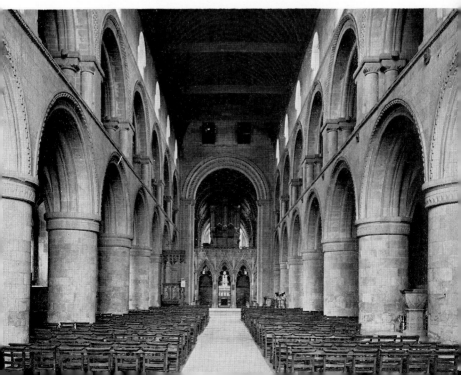

Tympanum on the west wall of the south porch, Church of St Mary, Malmesbury; *see* pp. 164–5 *(A. F. Kersting)*

Twelfth century 'Knights' from a pyx found at the Temple Church, London; *see* p. 107 *(Burrell Collection, Glasgow Art Gallery and Museum)*

Scholars began to concentrate at Oxford 'founding', so to speak, a university there. Two Englishmen, Adelard of Bath—tutor of the future Henry II—and Robert of Chester were among the first men responsible for the introduction of Arabic science to the West. Even the great magnates were, sometimes, patrons. The Winchester Bible was illuminated for Henry of Blois, while Geoffrey of Monmouth dedicated his *History* to Robert of Gloucester, prime trouble-maker in Stephen's reign.

England was now in effect a trilingual state. Clergy and officials wrote in Latin, though it was a Latin that had become infiltrated by a fifth column of English words, sometimes in a faintly classical disguise (*drana* for drain) but often unashamedly unaltered (*gingerbred*). The clergy were certainly able to preach in English and they, the officials and the courtiers normally spoke French. The common people interlarded their English with pidgin French. Thus the animals they looked after kept their Saxon names, but prepared for the lord's table, became French—*sheep* when alive were *mouton* (mutton) when dead, *cattle* become *boeuf* (beef), and so on.

The baronial reaction was favoured by special circumstances. On their accession both William II and Henry had faced rebellion—that was to be expected—but their hands had been strengthened by the fact that there was no disputed succession. Now matters were different. Although Henry had fathered at least twenty-one children only two of these were legitimate, Prince William and Matilda. In 1120 the White Ship, built to the latest pattern, struck a rock off Barfleur en route for England. The evidence indicates that virtually everyone on board was drunk and there was only one survivor, a butcher from Rouen. Prince William was among the drowned.

In 1127 Henry's remaining child, Matilda, came back to England. She had left the country when she was eight to be married to the Holy Roman Emperor. Now her husband was dead and she, aged twenty-five, was heir to the throne of England. Her father quickly forced her into a second diplomatic marriage, this time with Geoffrey of Blois, only fourteen years old but already the ruler of Anjou and Maine, territory that lay, conveniently, on the southern border of Normandy.

No one—except Henry—was pleased by the marriage. Matilda

in particular felt the ignominy that she, a dowager empress, should be married to a mere count. Nevertheless in 1133 she produced a son, the future Henry II. Two years later her father fell ill near Gisors having eaten far too many lampreys—a dish against which he had been expressly warned by his doctor. He died a week later and was buried at Reading in the monastery he himself had founded. The abbey was destroyed in the late eighteenth century and now only a few blackened stumps survive gloomily in Reading's public park, but a number of its remarkable carved capitals have been recovered—some of them from a marsh where they had been used as rubble to make a flood wall—and can be seen in the museum at Reading and in the Victoria and Albert Museum.

Matilda might have been expected to succeed to the throne, for in earlier days Henry had made the barons swear to accept her, but since then Henry's nephew Stephen had been treated by the King almost as an adopted son and had become the best-endowed baron in England or Normandy. Now he slipped quickly over to England and was crowned, as the chronicler Henry of Huntingdon put it, "in the twinkling of an eye".

It is difficult to decide whether or not this is what might have been expected of him, for Stephen's character was compounded of contradictions. William of Malmesbury described him as "an energetic man, but lacking in judgement, an active soldier at his best in a difficult situation, lenient to his enemies and courteous to all. Good at making promises, but not so good at keeping them". On the one hand he was suspicious, sly, inconstant and inclined to seize men while they were his guests. On the other hand there is evidence that in many ways he was like his uncle Robert Curthose, capable of acting with bravery, gallantry and generosity, and at least one contemporary thought him "too soft". Certainly these latter qualities were not ones that would make for success in twelfth-century Europe and Stephen's reign proved to be an anarchic disaster as barons seized the opportunity offered by a disputed succession to establish their hereditary rights.

In 1139 Matilda took advantage of the situation to invade England and here she remained until 1148, waging intermittent war from bases at Bristol and Gloucester. At first she won wide support, but her unsatisfied ambitions, combined no doubt with the natural ill-temper of all her family, had made her thoroughly disagreeable, greedy, proud and above all tactless so that now "beginning to walk and speak and do everything more arrogantly", she "behaved like an empress when she was not quite a queen"—behaviour that soon alienated many of her followers.

Stephen reacted energetically and the isolated castles of rebellious subjects were quickly forced to surrender. Traces of his siegeworks have survived at a number of places. At Exeter a chamber cut out of the rock on which the castle stands is believed to be the work of his engineers. At Corfe in Dorset traces of the siege can be seen in the very well-preserved earthworks still known as Stephen's Rings, a quarter of a mile to the south-west of the castle (SY/953820). Similar siegeworks are at Wallingford in Berkshire on the opposite bank of the Thames from the castle (SU/616906). In Sussex at Arundel there are a number of earthworks, some at least of which date from Stephen's reign, though others may represent an earlier siege in 1102; Cock Hill (TQ/089096), Warningcamp (TQ/028064), The Burgh (TQ/050126) and—the most impressive—Rackham (TQ/050126). Other works have been found at Hereford west of the cathedral, at Ludlow, and at Lincoln outside the west gate of the castle.

Unfortunately Stephen showed not only dash and determination but also a certain misplaced chivalry. At Lincoln in 1141 he abandoned a strong position and came down to level ground for a fair fight in which for his pains he was knocked down by a stone and captured. He had had a good day, though, fighting like a lion and breaking first a sword and then a Norwegian battle-axe in the process. Nevertheless Lincoln should have proved the end of his reign, but before the year was out he had been released in exchange for Matilda's half-brother, taken at Stockbridge.

And so the war went on, if only in a rather desultory way. As Henry of Huntingdon wrote wearily, "It was the King's custom to start many endeavours with vigour, but to bring few to a satisfactory conclusion". The situation was complicated by the intermittent descents of Matilda's son, the future Henry II. In 1142 he was brought over by his uncle and five years later he slipped over on his own but both attempts failed—indeed on the second occasion Stephen paid his passage back to Normandy. Eventually in 1153 Henry campaigned successfully and Stephen agreed to recognize him as his successor.

Within a year the King was dead and buried in the abbey he had founded at Faversham. At the dissolution of the monasteries the tomb was destroyed "for the trifling gain of the lead". Matilda's husband Geoffrey had died in 1151—there is a contemporary plaque in the Musée du Tessé at Le Mans—but Matilda lived on till 1167, spending an apparently pious old age on the Continent. At Ambazac, twelve miles north-east of Limoges on N714, there can be seen a piece of Byzantine material, the only surviving example of her many donations. She was buried at Bec (D130, south-east of Pont-Audemer) where, imperious to the last, she composed her own epitaph: "Here lies Henry's daughter, wife and mother, great by birth, greater by marriage, greatest by motherhood".

Throughout the years of civil war it was the local barons who kept the pot boiling and who were the sole beneficiaries. They were in the war for profit, they signed private non-aggression pacts among themselves, they plundered the towns and endowed monasteries with a percentage of their gains as an insurance against the dangers of the after-life. Above all, they built unlicensed castles—often nothing more than wooden towers, but potential centres of power. It appeared that England would suffer the sort of political fragmentation that bedevilled Germany.

Churches became fortresses. At Bampton in Oxfordshire Matilda's men put up a fortification, in the words of John of Worcester, "right on the church tower"; in 1141 the north tower at Exeter was battered during the siege—the damage can still be seen—and in that same year the cathedral at Lincoln was seized by the King and fortified. Two years earlier Worcester Cathedral had been crammed with refugees and looked, said an eye-witness, at once like a furniture-store and a common lodging-house, the sound of the service being drowned by the scream of children, and the clergy having to scramble over piles of sacks and chests.

The administrative machinery cracked under the strain; in 1148 an old knight lamented that "justice has fled and the laws are silenced". The social structure disintegrated, the *Anglo-*

Saxon Chronicle recording how "some, starving, ate the forbidden flesh of dogs and horses, while others ate raw grass and roots and villages stood almost deserted". The writer described in detail the misery in at least one area :

> When the traitors perceived that Stephen was a mild man and soft and good and did no justice, then did they all do terrible things . . . every powerful man made his castles and held them against him and they filled the land with castles. They oppressed greatly the wretched men of the land with the making of castles; when the castles were made, they filled them with devils and evil men. Then they seized those men, who they supposed had any possessions, both by night and by day, men and women, and put them into prison for their gold and silver and tortured them with unspeakable tortures. . . . They laid taxes on the villages and when the wretched men had no more to give, they robbed and burnt all the villages so that you might well go a whole day's journey and you would never find a man occupying a village, or land being tilled . . . the earth bare no corn, for the land was all ruined by such deeds; and men said openly that Christ and His saints slept. Such and more than we can say we endured for nineteen winters for our sins.

Of this multitude of 'adulterine', or unlicensed, castles scarcely any trace remains. Their wooden towers were taken and retaken, burnt and reconstructed, as necessity, greed or the shifting emphasis of baronial politics demanded, and with the end of the anarchy the majority were destroyed.

Some structures were more permanent, however, and it was at about this time that the palisade round the top of the motte was sometimes replaced by a stone wall, creating what is today known as a 'shell' keep. Occasionally this was built not as a free-standing wall but to revet the motte. Shell keeps are not easy to date, but many of them seem to have been put in the first half of the century. They can be well seen at Arundel in Sussex, Berkeley in Gloucestershire, Cardiff, Carisbrooke in the Isle of Wight, Farnham in Surrey, Tamworth in Staffordshire, Totnes in Devon and, much restored of course, at Windsor where the motte is itself 250 feet in diameter. There is a particularly good group in Cornwall at Launceston, Restormel (north of Lostwithiel) and at Trematon (west of Saltash and to the south of A38).

The motte even when revetted was rarely stable enough to support the weight of a decent stone residence and the practice began of setting-up a rectangular stone keep within the bailey and not on the motte itself. These keeps were high stone towers, modelled to some extent on those already in existence at Colchester and London, owing also something to examples in Normandy, where today the most satisfactory remains are those of the castle at Falaise.

There are about a dozen important 'great towers' of this period still to be seen, of which the key works are those at Norwich, Hedingham and Rochester. The keep at Norwich was a royal castle, built in the reign of Henry I. The outside was resurfaced in 1834-9 and the sharp carving is sometimes described as insensitive, but it probably gives a more accurate impression of what a castle looked like in its early days than that conveyed by romantically weathered stonework. The interior was gutted at the same time for use as a prison, but some twelfth-century details remain including a fireplace and part of the chapel, and the whole now houses a fine museum and art gallery.

Norwich was imitated in the private keep built about 1140 at Castle Rising (TF/666246, a few miles north of King's Lynn and west of A149). Although large it lies almost hidden by the high earth ramparts which closely surround it. The very plain walls are strengthened and made more interesting by pilaster buttresses, but the castle gives little away and so leaves one quite unprepared for the great stone staircase—the finest of its type—concealed in the forebuilding on its eastern side.

At Rochester Bishop Gundulf, the man responsible for the White Tower, raised a castle about 1088, but of his work only part of the wall round the keep still stands, for the castle was rebuilt about 1130 by the Archbishop of Canterbury, William of Corbeil. Matilda's half-brother Robert was imprisoned here after his capture at Stockbridge. Today it is still a huge structure, 70 feet square and rising through three storeys to a height of 113 feet. At the entrance the bar-hole and portcullis-slot are visible. The interior is divided in half by a cross-wall, pierced on the main floor by chevron-decorated arches and with a well-shaft built into it, while the upper floor is surrounded by a gallery-walk.

The tower keep at Hedingham in Essex (east of A604, Colchester–Cambridge), where Stephen's queen died in 1152, had been built by the Veres about 1140 and was in general a copy of Rochester. Its architecture marks the peak of these early twelfth-century towers and its interior has survived more completely than that of any other. Here one can get the best idea of what the rooms of a great twelfth-century household were like, especially the arched and galleried hall. The exterior gives a clear impression of the great strength of these tower-keeps, its walls still rising to a height of over a hundred feet. Here, as at Castle Rising, the entrance was protected by a forebuilding and though this has now gone the marks where it joined the main structure can be seen. The small cavities in the unscarred walls are putlog holes designed to hold scaffolding.

No other castles of this period are quite so impressive as those already mentioned, but there are several with interesting features of one sort or another. At Sherborne the hall-keep was built about 1120 by Roger, Bishop of Salisbury. Roger was originally a poor priest of Caen who owed his promotion to Henry I, pleased it is said by the speed with which he got through the Mass. Sherborne was not so much a castle as a strongly defended bishop's palace. The arrangements seem to have included a sort of cloister-walk round the buildings, but its walls were strong—so much so in fact that during the Civil War it held out for Charles I and when taken was 'slighted'—in effect, destroyed—by Fairfax. In consequence the main structure is almost gone but the south-west gatehouse still stands, four storeys high.

Corfe Castle has a rather similar history. The keep was added by Henry I about 1125 and was described a few years later as "one of the strongest in all England". When captured in the seventeenth century the defences were blown up by the Parliamentary forces, creating a ruin so picturesque that in its setting it is perhaps more satisfying than an untouched building would have been.

In Surrey there are castles at Farnham and Guildford. Of the former, built by 1138, the twenty-three-sided shell wall which surrounded the living quarters still stands, but the tower within was demolished in 1155. There is a good entrance staircase. Ten miles to the east at Guildford the grim rectangular keep, rather smaller than those already described, was put up against the side of the motte. It probably dates from the first half of the century, though work was carried out on it by Henry II—it was a royal castle—and the base has been restored in modern times.

At the royal castle of Lincoln there are two mottes. The more important was developed as a shell keep, the curtain wall was constructed by 1113, and the tower known as Lucy's Tower must date from before 1136 when Lucy, Countess of Chester, died. At Tamworth in Staffordshire the motte is very impressive —50 feet high with a diameter of 100 feet at the top. The herring-bone wall running up this dates from the time of Henry I, and the polygonal shell keep from the years after 1138.

Finally there is Old Sarum (SU/137237) an oddity just north of Salisbury on the Amesbury road (A345). Here an Iron Age fort housed a Norman castle and cathedral until the site was abandoned in the thirteenth century when a fresh cathedral was built at new Salisbury down by the river. At the time of the Conquest the Iron Age ditches were deepened, the ground within partially levelled and a motte raised at the centre—an unusual position made suitable by the fact that this was the highest point. The existing foundations are those of the royal castle built about 1130. This fell into decay after about 1270, and in the reign of Henry VIII "the stone walls and stones called the castle of Old Sarum" were granted to a certain Thomas Cowper, with liberty to knock them down and cart away the rubble. The cathedral which shared the enclosure was begun in William I's reign and enlarged by Roger of Salisbury, but there was always friction between the castellans and the canons, which was one of the reasons for the removal of the cathedral. Today the foundations can be well seen, but of the superstructure nothing remains except a capital, probably of imported stone, in the museum at new Salisbury.

By the end of Stephen's reign relations with both Scotland and Wales were determined, at least for the immediate future. At the death of the Conqueror the boundary between England and Scotland was still doubtful and it might have settled as far north as the Forth or as far south as the Tees on the east coast and the Ribble on the west, but in 1092 the capture of Carlisle by Rufus was followed by the *de facto* establishment of a boundary more or less as it exists today though both sides did not agree on it till 1237 and invasions, incursions and raids continued on both sides of the border until 1603. In 1138 Scottish forces ranged far south until decisively beaten at Cowton Moor north of Northallerton when the Scots army was "broken like a cobweb" and the men of Galloway "bristled with arrows like hedgehogs".

At peace or at war English influence was strong in southern Scotland and much of the best land passed into the hands of English exiles or Norman and Flemish adventurers. Among these was the family of Bruce from north Yorkshire, who became lords of Annandale, and Walter Fitz Alan, descended from an obscure Breton lord of Dol, who came north in 1141 and is the ancestor of the Stewarts. Scottish castles showing Norman influence are rare. The two best-authenticated are the tower at Sween near Knapdale in Argyle, said to be the oldest, and the shell keep at Rothesay in Bute.

In Wales the situation was more complex. The Conqueror had set up three earldoms over against the three ancient divisions of the country. In the north Hugh of Chester campaigned against Gwynedd, achieved great early successes—and then by 1098 had lost all the ground he had gained. In central Wales Roger of Shrewsbury, whose family name was Montgomery, drove deep into Powys and then pushed south-west to Cardigan and Pembroke, where a large colony of Flemings was settled about 1108. The third earldom, that of Hereford, made little progress until, in the reign of Henry I, Brecon and Glamorgan were occupied. Almost all the Norman gains were lost during the great national revival which began in 1136. In the north the Welsh pressed east, capturing Mold and threatening Chester itself. The Welsh guerrillas were more than a match for the Normans, as a Welshman observed: "The Normans seek flat grounds and fields, the Welsh the mountains and woods. To the Normans armour is an honour, to the Welsh an encumbrance. When the Normans capture knights they can be ransomed, but the Welsh cut off their heads". Only Pembrokeshire, 'little England beyond Wales', remained firmly under Norman control.

In consequence although almost 200 castles date from the twelfth century it is difficult to date them exactly for they were so often built, lost, recaptured, lost again. Those worth investigating include the following:

Brecknock (Brecon): twelfth-century shell keep or polygonal tower on motte.

Bronllys: SO/149346, A438 north-east from Brecon. Motte and bailey with round keep before 1175.

Tretower: SO/ 184212, A479, just beyond A40 fork. Motte and bailey, with shell keep and buildings. (The round tower is thirteenth century.)

Dolwyddelan (Caernarvonshire): SH/722523, A496, Bettws-y-Coed–Blaenau Ffestiniog. Rectangular keep 40 feet high with projecting stone corbels for a timber gallery. Late, but included as a Welsh-built keep and the birthplace of Llewelyn the Great (1194).

Carmarthen (Carmarthenshire): motte and bailey; twelfth-century shell keep revetting the motte.

Llanstephan: SN/351101, B4312 south-west from Carmarthen; round tower late twelfth century.

Cardiff (Glamorgan): motte of 1081, surmounted by a later twelve-sided shell wall, inside a square bailey formed by the walls of the Roman fort.

Coity: SS/923816, north-east of Bridgend on minor road; late twelfth-century rectangular keep within earlier ring-work.

Ogmore: SS/882769, B4524 south-west from Bridgend; rectangular stone keep (1130–40) and rectangular hall, all within ring-work.

Tomen-Y-Mur: (Merioneth): SH/705386, east of A487, Dolgellau–Portmadoc, opposite northern end of Llyn Trawsfynydd; motte (1090) within Roman fort.

Chepstow and Monmouth (Monmouth): see Chapter V.

White Castle: SO/380168, turn north off B4233, Abergavenny–Monmouth, at Llantilio Crossenny; motte with sandstone curtain wall (1163–88).

Pembroke (Pembrokeshire): round keep, an experimental improvement on the rectangular pattern, perhaps as early as 1185 (see p. 162).

The arrival of the Normans had given a fresh impetus to monasticism. Whereas in 1066 there were only about fifty monasteries in England, by 1100 the number had risen to 130, almost all of them Benedictine. At the same time the number of monks had increased dramatically; Gloucester, for instance, had only ten monks in 1066, but in 1104 there were over a hundred. The custom of linking monasteries with cathedrals, a largely English peculiarity, became at the same time much more common and by 1133 of seventeen cathedrals eight were monastic centres. Strictly these were cathedral-priories. A priory was technically an off-shoot of an abbey—thus all Cluniac foundations were priories, being under the Abbey of Cluny itself— and in these cathedral foundations the bishop stood in place of the abbot.

Numerous Benedictine churches are in use today, but the monastic buildings attached to them have either been destroyed or, as at some of the cathedrals, rebuilt at a later date. Rather fragmentary remains which are nevertheless of importance include some late work at the end of Glastonbury Abbey, Lindisfarne (see Chapter II) and Tynemouth. This last, founded about 1090 had a fearsome reputation. It was a daughter-priory of St Albans and a monk who had been sent there wrote to one of his old comrades: "Our house is on the top of a rock, surrounded on three sides by the sea. Day and night you can hear the breakers roaring and the thick sea mists make everything dark. There is no spring or summer, only a continual north wind and the cry of gulls. Take care not to come here." At Lastingham in the North Riding (north of A170, Thirsk–Pickering) there is a dramatically stark crypt dating from about 1088. In southern England the nave of Binham Priory in Norfolk (B1388, north of A148, Fakenham–Cromer), surrounded by the ruins of its monastic buildings, is in use as the parish church.

Nor are there many remains of the reformed Benedictine monasticism which had originated at Cluny. Although there were about thirty Cluniac priories in England there are only two or three places where their buildings can be seen today. Quite the most important is at Castle Acre in Norfolk (TF/830560, west of A1065, Swaffham–Fakenham), the ruins of which should not be missed. The west front is most exciting, every square foot being ornamented with arcading and carving. There are also considerable remains of the monastic buildings, but some of these are of later date. At Thetford in the same county (A11, Newmarket–Norwich) the ruins of the Cluniac priory have been excavated and here the east cloister range was built in the early part of the century. On the other side of England at Much Wenlock in Shropshire (south of Shrewsbury on A458 towards Bridgnorth) there is very fine arcading on the outer wall of the south transept, once the north wall of the chapter-house, and a free-standing octagonal stone basin, an unusual feature, at which the brethren washed their hands before and after meals.

The first half of the twelfth century saw the establishment in England of a number of new monastic orders. The most numerous were the Augustinians or Black Canons—colleges of priests living a communal life under the rule of St Augustine. By the end of the century they had 140 houses in England and Wales though many of these were small and poorly endowed. They were usually built in existing settlements and the nave or at least a part of it was used by the laity. In consequence at the Dissolution the monastic buildings usually disappeared—the land was valuable—but the nave was taken over by the community as the parish church and many of these are still in use.

The most exciting ruins are those of St Botolph's at Colchester which has also the distinction of being the first Augustinian house in England, built about 1100. The great round pillars of flint rubble and Roman brick are unlike any other remains and stand today like abstract works of sculpture. Among the churches still functioning there are a number of especial interest. In Cornwall at St Germans (SX/361572, south of A38 and west of Plymouth) the nave and aisle are early and there is a very good west doorway. At Christchurch in Hampshire the interior is almost unchanged, the nave, transepts and crypts all dating from the first half of the century, the exterior of the north transept and stair-turret being decorated with attractive blind arcading and diaper patterns.

Less impressive, but more dramatically situated, is St Mary's at near-by Portchester. Founded in 1133 by Henry I within the old Roman fort there was constant discord between the canons and the soldiers of Portchester Castle and about fifteen years later the Augustinians moved to Southwick, leaving behind a perfect little church. In Bedfordshire the nave of Dunstable Priory is all that survives of a much larger church built about 1150. The south aisle has been sensitively restored in the present century. To the east, on the outskirts of London is Waltham Abbey, a curiosity. The existing church is the nave—a superb piece of work second only to Durham—of the Norman church, about 120 feet in length. In 1177 Henry II reconstituted it is a priory of Augustinian canons as part of his atonement for the murder of Thomas Becket. In doing so he removed the eastern end of the Norman church and extended the abbey to the east in the form of an immense central nave 160 feet long, beyond this were wide transepts and beyond those a five-bayed presbytery in which was placed the tomb of King Harold. The abbey church was then 480 feet in length, comparable in size with Ely Cathedral. Today this has all gone and what one sees are only some of the foundations.

St Bartholomew's, Smithfield, was founded in 1123 by Henry I's jester Rahere, in thanks for his recovery from malaria when on pilgrimage to Rome. The eastern end is unchanged and includes a beautiful four-arched triforium and—a comparatively rare survival—the ambulatory or aisle round the apse. The tomb of Rahere himself is of later, Perpendicular, design.

During the century two reformed orders of Augustinians were established, the Gilbertines and the Premonstratensians. The former, founded about 1130 by Gilbert of Sempringham, were a double order for both sexes. There were never more than thirty houses and remains are rare, but at Old Malton in the North Riding, on A169 towards Pickering, the nave of the Gilbertine priory is now the parish church.

The Premonstratensians or White Canons were founded at Prémontré near Soissons and established in England in 1143. They have left one important ruin at Easby in the North Riding, off B6271 one mile east of Richmond. The site was restricted and this, together with problems of drainage, produced a very irregular and unusual lay-out, with the infirmary and the abbot's lodging placed on the north side of the church and reached by a passage from the north transept. The most impressive feature is the refectory which still stands two storeys high with the pulpit in its south wall from which readings were given at meal-times.

Very different were the military monastic orders, a by-product of the Crusades. The Knights Hospitallers of St John of Jerusalem, established to help sick, wounded and needy pilgrims to Palestine, did not reach England till about 1180, but the Knights Templars were established here by 1130. Their headquarters were in Jerusalem on the site of Solomon's Temple, their distinguishing mark a white cloak with a red cross, and until 1162 they consisted entirely of laymen living under the rule of the Cistercian order.

A number of round churches, consisting of a circular nave and a short choir and modelled on the Church of the Holy Sepulchre at Jerusalem, were founded in the west of Europe by these orders. Fifteen are known to have existed in England and four examples survive from the twelfth century. All are worth seeing, though all have suffered change. The best known is the Temple Church between Fleet Street and the Temple Gardens, which dates from 1186 and has been restored after being severely damaged in the Second World War. The other three churches date from the first half of the century. At Northampton the church of the Holy Sepulchre is an oddity, having had a nave and aisles added to the original round structure. The most picturesque is undoubtedly the ruined chapel in the grounds of Ludlow Castle in Shropshire which has particularly fine mouldings round the west doorway and on the chancel arch—the chancel itself has gone. The interior of Holy Sepulchre at Cambridge was restored in 1841 and though this was done quite sensitively much of the work is therefore not original.

It was the Cistercian order which made the greatest impact on twelfth-century England and which has left the most splendid ruins. This reformed Benedictine order had originated in 1098 at Cîteaux in Burgundy as a conscious reaction against the excessive ostentation of Cluny, for Cluniac monasticism, like so many reform movements, had itself become arrogant and worldly, features well-illustrated by the third rebuilding of Cluny itself. That work was begun in 1088 and resulted in the creation at Cluny of a huge concourse of buildings around a church with a nave—which Henry I helped to complete—no less than 450 feet in length. The monastery was destroyed after the Revolution and almost all that remains today is a part of the transept, terrifying in its immensity, and a handful of splendid carvings in the granary, now a museum.

The new movement owed much of its driving force to that autocratic inflexible Puritan St Bernard of Clairvaux (1115-53). It dominated the period, reaching England in 1128 and establishing sixty-three communities during the century.

The Cistercian emphasis was on simplicity and hard work. Thus the Benedictines and the Cluniacs dyed the wool for their habits, they were 'black monks', but the Cistercians used undyed wool, they were 'white monks'. Scholarship was not essential—"Labour is prayer"—and a characteristic of the order was the division into monks and lay-brothers. The latter lived under the same rule but in their own part of the monastery and ran the estates. They need not be literate—indeed in 1256 lay-brothers were expressly forbidden to have books. Normally they greatly outnumbered the monks, at Rievaulx there were about 150 monks and 600 lay-brothers. Yet the community was a single unit and in the second half of the century a Cistercian could write "We devote ourselves to the field-work which God created; we all work together, we and our lay-brethren and our hirelings, each according to his ability; and all in common we live on our labour."

Simplicity was explicit in their architecture. St Bernard attacked buildings of "excessive length, unnecessary breadth, expensive finish and strange designs"—a direct hit at Cluny. In consequence the churches were as small as possible—there was no question of the laity using the building—square-ended with no eastern chapels or apse, with a plain nave, originally aisle-less, and perhaps a narrow western porch, a good example of which survives at Fountains. When aisles were added they were only passages, cut off from the nave by stone screens against which were built the stalls of the lay-brothers. There was no bell tower for there were no great bells, but only a low tower over the crossing. The towers at Rievaulx and Fountains, so conspicuous today, are very late additions.

St Bernard wrote even more strongly about the decoration of monasteries:

What profit is there in those ridiculous monsters, in deformed beauty, beautiful deformity? What is the use of those obscene monkeys, roaring lions, centaurs, tigers, knights and hunters. Here are many bodies with a single head, there one body with

many heads. . . . We look more at the stone-work than at the
service book . . . if men are not ashamed by this rubbish they
should at least blush at the expense. . . . We walk on sacred figures;
here the face of an angel is spat upon, there the face of a saint
vanishes beneath the feet of passers-by.

Another writer comments "Adam and Eve are warm on our
church walls, but the poor huddle naked in the winter cold."

In consequence, the first Cistercian monasteries are distinguished by an austere architecture, the only applied ornamentation being on the capitals where it is restricted to very simple,
very beautiful, leaf-forms, together with a certain amount of
Romanesque moulding round the doorways and windows,
which in general were arched in the semi-circular manner,
though the Burgundian influence of Cîteaux shows itself in the
early adoption of the more 'modern' pointed arch for the vaulting in the aisles, the earliest examples being at Rievaulx and
Kirkstall (1152). The interior was white-washed, the joints in
the stonework being picked out with red lines and—sometimes
—a small formalized red flower might be allowed in each
rectangle.

The Cistercians deliberately set up their communities in
lonely places and in consequence the remains of their buildings
have survived more completely—and more picturesquely—than
those of any other order. They began to build in Stephen's reign
and though work continued throughout the century the style
alters little and in consequence seems to belong in essence to the
early years.

The first community was established at Waverley in Surrey,
but here only a few stones stand, the earliest work of any consequence being at Rievaulx and dating from 1132. This is earlier
than anything in France, where the oldest remains (1139) are
at Fontenay (off N5 between Auxerre and Dijon) where there
is buried the retired Bishop of Norwich, Everard, who began the
work.

The general monastic plan varied little from place to place or
from order to order. Benedictine, Cluniac, Cistercian, Augustinian—all built to the same pattern which was itself dictated not
so much by tradition as by fitness for purpose. The description

which follows therefore, though based mainly on the Cistercian monastery of Rievaulx, can in general be applied to any monastic site.

Most obviously, that site had to be close to running water, essential not only for the preparation of food and drink but also for milling and sanitation. (An exception is Battle Abbey, evidence that it was indeed built to mark the spot where Harold fell.) The water supply was always carried under the buildings by a carefully engineered web of pipes and drains, the latter providing the basis for later stories of underground passages.

There were four essentials; the church, the living quarters, the buildings devoted to the sick and old, and those for day-to-day activities involving the outside world. The church itself ran, where possible, east and west, but at Rievaulx it had to be placed almost north and south. The main monastic buildings lay to the south of the church and formed with it a rectangular area, the cloister, surrounded by a cloister walk normally about ten feet wide. The arcading which sheltered this walk usually dates from later centuries, but there is a good eleventh-century section in the east walk of the infirmary cloister at Canterbury. The beginning of the east wall of the cloister was formed by the exterior of the south transept of the church. In this there is often a shallow recess, all that remains of the cupboard in which books were stored for work in the sunny north cloister which served as the *scriptorium*, and beside this at Rievaulx there was a narrow room containing the rest of the library— a feature typical of Cistercian monasteries—and behind it the vestry.

Next came the chapter-house, where the business of the day was arranged, duties allocated and punishments decreed. After the church itself this was in many ways the most important of the monastic buildings for here the community acted, feeling itself a corporate unit. There are particularly good chapter-houses at Fountains and Jervaulx. Next to the chapter-house was the parlour, originally a narrow passage where there was permission to talk (*parler*) but eventually developed as a small room. Then at Rievaulx came the treasury, day-stairs from the dormitory above, and a passage (*slype*) leading to a large group of buildings east of the cloister and south of the church. There is a very fine twelfth-century *slype*, still in use, at Gloucester.

This ground floor of the east range is often referred to as the *sub-dorter* for the whole of the first floor above it was occupied by the dormitory (*dortor*) which ran from the south transept due south. It usually extended beyond the cloister—at Rievaulx it was over a hundred yards in length. Since the monks had to leave their beds at about midnight for Matins it was essential that the dormitory should adjoin the church and from one end a night stair led down into the south transept itself. The best such stair to have survived is in the former Augustinian Priory at Hexham, now the parish church.

Attached to the dormitory there was always a lavatory, or *reredorter*, usually placed at the south end or, as at Rievaulx, about halfway down the eastern side of the dormitory. It contained a row of wooden seats, sometimes separated by partitions, built above a stream of running water. At Canterbury there was 'seating' for fifty-five, and the stone-work of a twelve-seater is well-preserved at Castle Acre.

The south side of the cloister was composed of a warming room, a refectory (*frater*) and the kitchens. In most orders the refectory ran east and west thus occupying the whole of this side, but in the second half of the twelfth century the Cistercians found it more practical to run it at right angles, as at Rievaulx. In this way they saved space and were able to place the kitchen where it could serve the refectory of the monks on one side and a separate refectory for the lay-brothers on the other. Here it was provided with service-hatches and turntables.

On either side of the refectory door at Rievaulx there were lead-lined troughs where the monks washed their hands before and after meals. At this time there were no forks, fingers being used instead, and the *laver* was an important feature. At Durham it was recorded that "within the cloister over against the refectory was a fair *laver* for the monks to wash their hands and faces at, made in round form covered with lead and all marble except the walls, with twenty-three taps of brass . . . and on either side of the *laver* was a cupboard, kept always with sweet and clean towels for the monks to dry their hands".

146

The refectory was a large room—at Rievaulx it measured 124 feet by 38 feet and at Fountains 110 feet by 47—with a pulpit half-way down the west side from which the monks were read to during their silent meals. There is a good example at Fountains, and at Beaulieu, where the refectory has become the church, the thirteenth-century pulpit is still in use.

In most orders the west side of the cloister was a general-purpose block. Here was the great store house (cellarium) for the monastic supplies of all kinds and here too might be guest-rooms and sometimes the abbot's quarters. But in the Cistercian order it contained, in addition to the store-rooms, the refectory and the dormitory of the lay-brothers. At Rievaulx this range is curiously small and unimpressive, but at Fountains it is very fine and the undercroft beneath the lay-brothers' dormitory is the largest in Europe, being 100 yards long. Originally it was divided by a cross-wall into two parts, the northern section housing the cellarer's stores, the southern part being the lay-brothers' refectory. From the northern end of the lay-brothers' dormitory a stair and door led into the west end of the nave. This doorway, though not the stair, can be seen at Rievaulx.

The buildings which made up the four sides of the cloister thus represented the institutional heart of the monastery, but in area they were exceeded by subsidiary buildings required for daily life. These did not require a fixed plan and were arranged as the lie of the land dictated, but in general to the west of the church was the gate-house, some sort of guest-house and chapel for the laity, and, as at Fountains, the mill, bakehouse, brewhouse, fishponds and so on, all lying within a precinct wall. This last has usually disappeared but at Bury St Edmunds there is a good example of a Romanesque gatehouse together with a length of wall, while at Battle Abbey no less than 700 feet of wall still stands on the north side.

East of the cloister and reached by the slype were often the abbot's quarters and almost always the infirmary, away from the bustle of everyday life. The infirmary, which served not only the ill but also the old and those who had received the periodic blood-letting, was an important feature of most monasteries. At Rievaulx it is represented by a large hall 145 feet by 33 feet standing on the east side of its own cloister, while at Fountains the infirmary hall is even bigger, measuring together with the chapel at its east end 170 feet by 70 feet. At Ramsey (on B1040, north of Huntingdon) the infirmary is now in use as the parish church.

Within this comparatively rigid arrangement of buildings the monks followed an equally rigid pattern of life. The exact details varied from order to order and indeed from summer to winter, but the general time-table was everywhere much the same. At midnight the monks rose from their beds and went down the night stairs into the church to sing Matins and Lauds, after which they went back to the dormitory until their day began at six with the short service of Prime. For this they dressed in their day clothes and afterwards washed and then ate a light meal (*mixtum*) consisting of four ounces of bread and a third of a pint of beer or wine. At nine a low mass and the short service of Terce was said, followed by the daily meeting in the chapter-house. Then there was work until noon when the office of Sext and a High Mass was sung after which the community ate the main meal of the day, consisting of bread, soup, fish or eggs, and cheese and fruit. On Sundays and festivals this was preceded by a procession through the church. The exact positions which the monks took up in the nave during the saying of the bidding prayers can still be seen marked by limestone slabs at Fountains and by incised circles in the stone flags at Easby. Next came the office of Nones and a period of work or recreation until Vespers at six. After that came a light supper, the shore service of Compline, and bed about nine.

There is no doubt that the best place in which to envisage the daily life of a twelfth-century monk is in the ruins of a Cistercian monastery. There are interesting sites in the North Riding at Byland, Jervaulx and Rievaulx; in the West Riding at Fountains, Kirkstall and Roche; in Shropshire at Buildwas; in Lancashire at Furness, and in Wales at Cwmhir and Strata Florida.

Byland: (1177) south of A170, Thirsk–Helmsley, and about two miles west of Ampleforth. The church is large—330 feet long—and late, and there are signs that the massive Puritanism of the early days was giving place to the fastidious grace of the next period. There was carving on the capitals picked out in red; notice the green and yellow tiling still in place in the south transept, and the niche of the book cupboard in the north-east corner of the cloister.

Jervaulx: (*c.* 1156–75) east of A6108, Ripon–Leyburn. The best preserved parts are the monastic buildings.

Rievaulx: (1132) west of B1257 and four miles north of Helmsley. One of the best; the surroundings, including the pleasantly eccentric Rievaulx–Terraces, were landscaped by Sir Charles Duncombe in the eighteenth century.

Fountains: (1135) south of B6265 from Ripon. The finest of all, standing pink and grey in scenery that was 'improved' in the eighteenth century to the instructions of John Aislabie, but which presented a very different appearance when a prior and twelve monks left the Benedictine abbey of York to come to a "place remote from all the world, uninhabited, set with thorns, and among the hollows of mountains with sharp rocks on every side, more suitable it seemed for the dens of wild beasts than for the use of men". The nave, west porch and doorway are early, the tower is late. Notice especially the undercroft beneath the lay-brothers' dorter, the chapter-house, refectory, infirmary hall and chapel, and the ninety yards of stone tunnels providing water and drainage.

Kirkstall: (1142) on A65 north from central Leeds. The chapter-house is well-preserved.

Roche: (*c.* 1170) south of A634, Rotherham–East Retford, and two miles south-east of Maltby. The transepts still stand and some foundations of the monastic buildings can be traced. In the eighteenth century the site was landscaped by 'Capability' Brown.

Buildwas: (1148) south of B4380, off A5 a little east of Shrewsbury and south of B4380 towards Iron Bridge. The best preserved part is the nave with fine cylindrical pillars, and the chapter-house. Unusually, the cloister is placed north of the church, because of the river.

Cwmhir: (1143) in Radnor SO/056715, west of A483, Builth-Wells–Newtown. Take the minor road one mile north of Crossgates. A typically lonely setting.

Strata Florida: (1166) in Cardigan; take B4343, Devil's Bridge–Tregaron, and then a minor road to the east seven miles north of Tregaron. Minimal ruins, but a lovely west doorway.

Furness: (1127) north-east of Barrow-in-Furness. The surviving portions are really too late for this book, being early thirteenth century, but the style is still Romanesque and it would be a pity to miss the five superb doorways to the chapter-house and, in general, the contrast between the red stone and the green landscape.

VII

THE REIGN OF HENRY II
1154—1189

The new king was overflowing with restless energy. It was said that he never sat down except when he was eating or hunting and that even in church he could not stop talking. His enemy Louis VII complained that he was "now in Ireland, now in England, now in Normandy; he must fly rather than travel by horse or ship". A courtier, Peter of Blois, wrote, "if the king had announced that he was going to stay all day, he was certain to leave early in the morning. If on the other hand he ordered an early start, he was equally certain to remain where he was till mid-day. I hardly dare say so, but I think he did it on purpose."

Twenty-one years old when he came to the throne, Henry was of medium height, stocky and tending to run to fat, red-haired and freckled, with protuberant grey eyes. He was given to uncontrollable rages and then those eyes would become suffused with blood and that face purple, and it was said that he would lie on the floor and bite the rushes with which it was covered. His fair was unfashionably short and so was his cloak, in the Angevin style, so that men called him Curtmantle. His hair and his cloak were alike expressions of his love of efficiency —though men attributed the former to his fear of going bald.

His reign was, as one might expect, marked by great success —and great failure: success in material affairs, failure in personal matters. The story of his love-hate relationship with Becket is characteristic. For seven years Henry worked closely with Thomas Becket, a middle-class Norman, tall and thin, some fifteen years older than the King. Appointed Chancellor in 1155 he proved himself another Henry, a man of extremes who did everything with committed thoroughness and to observers he seemed to be "not only the King's friend, but also, at it were, his master". Then, in 1162, the King chose Becket to succeed to the Archbishopric of Canterbury, the Pope approved—and the secular royal servant became at once the ardent defender of the rights of the Church against the demands of the State.

The breach was absolute. Becket soon went into a self-imposed exile. Then in 1170 he returned to Canterbury determined to assert the Church's claims. Henry heard the news in France and "burning with anger he again and again cursed those who owed all to him and yet would not avenge him on that one priest". Four knights took him at his unconsidered word and, crossing the Channel, cut down the Archbishop in the north transept of his cathedral. Today a tablet marks the spot. It was a martyrdom which caught the imagination of Europe. Three years later Becket was canonized and within a very short time his cult extended from Scandinavia to Sicily, from Castile to Acre.

After the murder Henry went campaigning in Ireland, hoping perhaps that meanwhile the hullabaloo would die down a little. He had in 1155 obtained from Pope Hadrian IV—an Englishman, indeed the only English Pope—the Bull *Laudabiliter*, authorizing the conquest of Ireland. Henry did not remain long in the island but from now on there was intermittent activity for fifty years and by 1215 two-thirds of the island had been occupied by colonists not only from England, but also from Wales, Scotland and France. Everywhere these new men put up the familiar motte-and-bailey and the sites of over 130 have been identified. Usually only the earthworks remain, but there is early stonework at Carrickfergus (Antrim) and Dundrum (Down) in Northern Ireland, and at Athlone (Westmeath), Carlingford (Louth), Maynooth (Kildare), Nenagh (Tipperary) and Trim (Meath) in Eire.

In 1172 Henry received absolution from the papal legates for his part in the murder of Becket, but that was not the end of its repercussions. The murder had occurred at a time when Henry was involved in another feud, less well known but longer drawn out—that with his wife and his sons.

In 1152 he had, in a whirlwind affair, married Eleanor of Aquitaine, divorced two months earlier from her unsatisfactorily passive husband Louis VII of France. Aquitaine comprised the whole south-western quarter of France. At a stroke Henry had extended his lands to such effect that they now stretched from the Cheviots to the Pyrenees; he was King of England, Duke of Normandy, Count of Anjou and Maine, and Duke of Aquitaine. The marriage may not have been so cold-blooded as this suggests for Eleanor was not only a great heiress, she was also immensely attractive.

> If the world were mine
> From sea to Rhine,
> I'd give it all
> If Eleanor would fall
> And lie with me.

sang the wandering scholars. Unfortunately she had other qualities. She was as self-willed as Henry—and eleven years older.

At first all went well, but in 1165 Eleanor left for Aquitaine and, apart from a brief visit to England in 1167, she was in France from 1168 to 1174, her energies largely devoted to the work of encouraging her sons to revolt against their father—not a difficult task, for they had inherited a full measure of the characteristic Norman-Angevin family disloyalty. Again there was a failure of personal relationships in which Henry played his part. He would grant to his sons—Henry, Richard, Geoffrey and John—revenue and titles in his far-flung empire, but never the authority which Eleanor and the King of France—who knew very well what he was about—constantly if unobtrusively encouraged them to demand.

From 1173 till his death in 1189 Henry faced almost constant rebellion from one or more of his family. Late in his reign the King is described as staring at a fresco at Winchester, which showed four young eagles attacking an old one, and then observing with a certain gloomy satisfaction: "Those eaglets are my sons who are harrying me to death." He was not alone in his views. When the eastern Patriarch Heraclius was on a visit to England he declared forthrightly "they came from the Devil and to the Devil they will go".

In 1173 the first rebellion occurred, the only one that affected England directly. In the late summer of that year the King of

Scotland, William the Lion, invaded northern England and almost immediately revolt broke out in East Anglia led by the Earls of Leicester and Norfolk. Their forces were soon augmented by Flemish mercenaries, said to number 14,000, despatched by the Count of Flanders to support, at least in theory, the claims of Prince Henry, the king's eldest son. They came over singing

> We have not come to stay
> But to destroy old Henry,
> We'll have his wool. . . .

—for many of them were weavers—and, even more optimistically, they told one another,

> Hop, hop, Willykin, hop,
> England is mine and thine,

but they were in fact easily routed near Bury St Edmunds. A contemporary wrote "the knights knocked them down and the peasants finished them off".

In spite of the Flemish fiasco, in the next campaigning season the situation grew worse for the royal forces. Henry, in a characteristic burst of energy, now took a hand himself. On 8th July he landed at Portsmouth and, having despatched Eleanor to prison at Salisbury, five days later he was in Canterbury Cathedral submitting to a dramatic scourging by the monks, followed by a night on the ground before the Martyr's tomb, naked "without even a carpet or anything else under him". Then he left for London where, four days later, he heard the news that the King of Scots had been defeated and captured at Alnwick on the very day that he had completed his penance. His prayer "St Thomas, guard my kingdom for me" had been answered. Fizzing with vigour and confidence he rode off to capture Huntingdon—his siege works can still be seen by the millstream, 400 yards west of the castle motte (TL/241715)—and within a week, under the impact of these various pressures, political, military and, apparently supernatural, the rebellion had collapsed.

Henry had proved one too many for his assorted enemies. From 1175 to 1182 he was at the height of his power and was able to devote a comparatively large part of his time to England.

The King of Scots, housed briefly in Richmond castle, was now shipped to Falaise, while Henry added "by the grace of God" to his royal style and began a carefully planned programme of castle-building and confiscation. In France his troubles continued, kept alive by his son Richard, by the King of France, and by such men as Bertran de Born, who sang—for he combined the activities of troubadour and professional trouble-maker—

> I love
> Not wine nor food nor rest, but still to fight
> And see death march with fire and sword.

In England, however, there was peace and firm government— the foundation of the English legal system date from this time —and here it is the royal castle and the parish church which symbolize his reign.

On his accession Henry's immediate objective had been to destroy the adulterine castles which had sprung up like toadstools, to recover control over royal castles that had been alienated and, whenever a chance offered itself, to reduce by confiscation or destruction the number of legitimate, licensed baronial castles. It was a policy that he continued to pursue throughout his reign and one that was to be followed later by his youngest son John. In 1154 there were in existence about 225 baronial castles and forty-nine royal ones, a ratio of almost five to one; sixty years later there were 179 baronial castles and ninety-three royal ones, the ratio was now rather less than two to one.

This decisive shift in the balance of power was the result of steady, nagging, niggling pressure throughout the years, supplemented by three periods of concentrated activity; the restoration of order after Stephen's reign (1154–8), the aftermath of the rebellion (1174–8), and the years 1208 to 1214—a function of King John's general policy of attempting to strengthen the monarchy at the expense of its great subjects

In the course of these years some castles changed hands more than once, the important castles of Appleby and Brough, for instance, passing from royal to baronial control and back again no less than five times in the half century after their acquisition from the King of Scotland in 1157.

Although the pattern dates from the first years after the Conquest it is to this period that the majority of the most impressive, the most typical Norman castles belong, those rectangular stone towers that still dominate their surroundings. The main development is that these later examples tend in general to be noticeably loftier in proportion to their bulk.

The transition from the motte-and-bailey of earth and timber to the rectangular stone keep is largely concentrated within Henry II's reign, the King himself being involved in a widespread and practically continuous building programme which reached its peak in the 'seventies. The average yearly outlay was almost £800 and represented the largest call on an annual revenue of less than £10,000. Although the greatest individual outgoings were on frontier castles, the major part of the overall expenditure was devoted to the strengthening of two or three dozen castles in the interior of the kingdom.

The consequence of all this activity was that by the end of the century there were few if any royal castles without stonework of some sort, though their permanent garrisons were sometimes ridiculously small, numbering perhaps less than a dozen men, skeleton staffs rather than military police, their business to keep the castle in working order. The larger castles functioned as court residences, administrative quarters for royal officials, and centres of local government that could be used as treasuries and prisons, their day-to-day maintenance being the responsibility of the sheriffs, acting under royal supervision.

Expenditure was particularly heavy on work at Newcastle (1168–78) and Dover (1180–90), and only a little less so on the towers at London, Windsor, Winchester, Scarborough and Orford. At Dover the total was about £7,000—for comparison, Richard I's show castle of Château Gaillard cost only £4,000—the effect of which was to create a perfect example of the twelfth-century keep in its most sophisticated form. Dover evolved directly from the White Tower of a century earlier and it marks the end of that line of development for by the time it was finished it was, as will be seen, already obsolete.

It is a difficult structure to envisage in its Henrician shape since Dover was for centuries the key to Britain and in consequence has undergone continual building and rebuilding. It is the keep and inner curtain wall that date from this period. The wall is hung from fourteen square open-backed towers, those on the north-eastern and southern sides being paired to form strong gate-houses. The keep is a cube, 95 feet by 96 feet, containing four floors on each of which the central area is divided by a cross-wall, while a nest of rooms occupies the strong outer walls, 17 feet thick at their base. The keep was provided with two chapels, one on either side of the entrance stairway, and a well over 240 feet deep fed a sophisticated plumbing system consisting of a network of lead pipes three inches in diameter. Here, too, the first true arrow-slits make their appearance—these can be distinguished from other slit openings by the fact that a downward splay was necessary if they were to be of any use for defensive purposes.

At Newcastle, the strategic key to the north, Robert Curthose had put up a castle on his way back from the Scottish campaign of 1080. Now, a century later, Henry built a new keep, rising to a height of 80 feet. Here, more easily than at Dover, a sophisticated great tower can be examined, though it must be admitted that its position overlooking the railway tends to baulk the historical imagination.

An open stairway leads to the entrance on the second floor, passing on the right a guard-room in the forebuilding, to reach the heart of the castle, a hall surrounded by a stone gallery. On the south side is a large room, now called 'the King's room', with a fireplace and attached garderobe, while in the south-east corner of the hall a spiral staircase leads up to another floor and to the battlements. It also leads down to the lower floor and a postern exit. In this way daily comings and goings could be excluded from the hall and there was the additional advantage that, if an enemy should carry the main staircase, defenders on the battlements could by-pass the area and either make their escape or, alternatively, re-enter by the main staircase and take the enemy in the rear.

Back in the main hall there is a well chamber in the north-east corner with a stone-lined well 99 feet deep from which pipes led to other parts of the castle. Below this floor there is a second hall and chamber and below that again the store-room, which could only be reached from inside the castle, while in the fore-building, below the guard-room, is the chapel. In the walls on the west side there were garderobes at all levels. The whole complex, inter-locking pattern was self-contained. All that was needed for a successful resistance was food—and this need not be very elaborate. At the small Northumberland castle of Wark the defenders were provided with oatmeal and malt, and on this diet of beer and porridge a garrison of fifty men in 1174 successfully defied the King of Scotland and his army.

Henry acquired Scarborough castle in 1155 and here on its superb site, a triangular peninsula overlooking the North Sea and separated from the mainland by a deep ditch, he rebuilt the existing keep and added the curtain walls (the bridge and barbican which protected the western approach are thirteenth-century). The new keep conformed to the new pattern, four storeys high with the entrance on the second storey from which separate staircases led up and down, the whole provided with fireplaces and garderobes. This castle was slighted by the Parliamentary forces in 1645 so that today most of the west wall has gone, but the first storey is complete and above that the destruction has left a useful cross-section through the upper levels.

Henry's great keep at Richmond has a different history, since it is not a new structure but an example of make-do-and-mend, for it was formerly the gatehouse. The castle was confiscated by the King in 1171 and a new entrance was made to the east of the gatehouse. The old entrance was then blocked off and the gatehouse transformed into a keep 100 feet high, reached on the second storey by a door in its south-east corner. As usual the entrance hall had to be crossed in order to ascend another stair, built in the thickness of the south wall, to the third storey and the battlements. The second and third storeys each consist of a large room with mural chambers at either end; there are some graffiti in the eastern chamber on the second floor. On the ground floor an impressive octagonal pillar stands over the well and supports the floor above.

Since the rectangular keeps were strictly functional their general pattern was uniform, though it might vary in detail. The entrance was never at ground level, but was reached by a stair, either open or enclosed in a forebuilding, which also often contained the guardroom and a chapel. The stair led straight into the main room and this, like the main rooms above and below it, was often divided by a cross-wall which carried the floor beams, for the upper floors were invariably of wood. Small rooms and garderobes were built into the thickness of the walls; the latter can usually be distinguished by the fact that they do not open directly into the main room, but are reached by a short passage. There is almost always a well and the main rooms are supplied with fireplaces, but there is never a proper kitchen. The ground-floor, accessible only from within the keep, was the store-room and on occasion may have made a convenient place in which to keep prisoners but stories of its regular use as a prison should be discounted.

If all this sounds austere, it must be remembered that the accommodation was normally supplemented by domestic buildings within the inner bailey, including a hall. These have usually disappeared or are, as at Ludlow, of later date, but it is always worth keeping a look-out for signs of their former existence, while the refectory of a monastery and the abbot's quarters help to piece out the picture of a great lord's accommodation. Of twelfth-century secular buildings one must make do with one survivor and a few fragments. The survivor is the late twelfth-century hall at Oakham in Rutland, measuring 65 feet by 43 feet, with fine stone arches dividing the floor space into a nave and two aisles. Every peer who passes through has to pay a toll of a horseshoe and these decorate the walls. The fragments include the hall in the bailey at Christchurch, which lacks only the timber floors and the roof, but has been much restored; at Framlingham (*see below*) the east curtain wall has interesting remains of fireplaces and chimney-stacks, and at Durham there is an elaborately moulded doorway leading to the Bishop's Hall in the castle.

None of these are royal. Those have all gone, unless one includes Westminster Hall, built for Rufus, who characteristically commented that it was "not half big enough—too large for a room, too small for a hall", but which, as it stands today, was virtually rebuilt later. There is written evidence, however, that royal residences were places of some comfort, surrounded by gardens, dovecots and fishponds, kitchens and mews—although their windows were still filled with 'linen cloth'.

Rectangular keeps of this period include the following:

Bamburgh (Northumberland): B1341, east off A1 between Alnwick and Berwick; the keep, in a fine position overlooking the sea, was probably begun during Stephen's reign. It was acquired by Henry II in 1157 and improved in the 'sixties; there are four storeys, extensively restored.

Brough (Westmorland): A66, twenty-one miles south-east of Penrith; first acquired by Henry II in 1157, it changed hands a number of times; the keep, which stands on a Roman foundation within the Roman fort, was reconstructed by Henry after its re-acquisition by the Crown in 1173.

Brougham (Cumberland): A66 just east of Penrith; built about 1175; four storeys, the fourth rebuilt about 1300.

Goodrich (Hereford): SO/577200, B4229, three miles south-west of Ross-on-Wye; in royal hands by 1177; a most impressive red sandstone tower, its original entrance later converted into a window; slighted in the seventeenth century.

Kenilworth (Warwickshire): A46 south-west of Coventry; a complex site, its buildings covering the whole period 1155–1649; the rectangular keep 'Caesar's Tower', represents Henry's work, its north wall was slighted in the seventeenth century.

Ludlow (Shropshire): A49, Shrewsbury–Leominster; one of the finest baronial castles, Ludlow is another complex structure including something of every century from the eleventh to the sixteenth. In particular, the inner curtain wall and its towers date from about 1090, while the domestic buildings on the north-west side of the inner bailey are from the thirteenth and fourteenth centuries. The twelfth-century features are the much-ruined outer curtain wall, the round chapel (see p. 142), and the rectangular keep on the south side. As at Richmond, this was constructed, in the second half of the century, out of the former gatehouse, the old entrance being blocked up and a new gateway made through the wall just to the east. Ludlow was in royal hands during the greater part of the period 1177–1215.

Middleham (North Riding): A6108, nineteen miles north-east of Ripon; a baronial keep, built after 1170 and one of the largest in England, measuring 100 feet by 80 feet; enclosed by a ditch, it has two main storeys and at ground level the space is divided by a cross-wall, the eastern division having a vaulted roof supported on five impressive columns.

Norham (Northumberland): B6470, west off A698 from Berwick; rebuilt later than 1157, it was in royal hands 1174–89; guarding a ford over the Tweed, it stood 90 feet high, but is now in a ruinous condition.

Peveril, or Peak (Derbyshire): at Castleton on A625, Whaley-Bridge–Sheffield; acquired by the Crown about 1153, the keep dates from about 1175 (*see also* p. 110).

Portchester (Hampshire): south of A27, Portsmouth–Farnham; an impressive keep in the north-west corner of the Roman fort; its height was increased from two to four storeys after it passed into royal hands in 1174—the change is clearly marked by the windows and buttresses.

While the rectangular keep appeared to have reached a form which could not be improved upon, it had a serious weakness —the corners could be brought down by sapping. To do this a gallery, supported by timber was driven under the corner, the wood was then fired and the corner collapsed, exposing the interior. The whole operation was made easier by the fact that it was difficult for the defenders to cover these blind corners with their weapons.

At Bungay in Suffolk a gallery of this type has been found under the south-west corner, dug in 1176 on Henry II's orders to destroy the keep which had been surrendered at the close of the great rebellion. At Rochester one corner of the keep is round, not square. It was here that the original work was mined when the castle was besieged by John in 1215, a tunnel being driven as described above, after which, according to the Rolls Series, "forty of the fattest pigs of the sort least good for eating" were used to fire the props. On this occasion the garrison held out for some time beyond the interior cross-wall, but after the siege had lasted for seven weeks the castle was taken and then, wrote Roger of Wendover, "few cared to put their trust in castles". In fact new types of fortification were coming into use by that time and the old tower keep was already out of date.

Various attempts were made to solve the problem. One of the simplest was to enclose the corners with large, solid, clasping buttresses, as at Kenilworth. But there were more imaginative experiments, largely derived from the experience of the Crusaders in the eastern Mediterranean area where the development of

L   161

projectile engines such as the trebuchet, which could hurl stones weighing half a hundredweight, made it necessary to develop patterns of wall surface off which the projectiles might skid. A cylindrical tower was one solution. Quite the most impressive and complete example in Britain is the round tower of Pembroke Castle, 75 feet high and 20 feet thick at its base, erected about 1200 by William Marshal. At about the same date a keep was put up at Helmsley in the North Riding which had three straight sides and a curved one.

But a quarter of a century earlier two more interesting experiments, which can still be seen today, had already been carried out, at Orford and Conisbrough. Orford (1165–73) in Suffolk stands at the end of B1084, east of A12, Ipswich–Lowestoft, and was built to discourage Hugh Bigod, Earl of Norfolk and one of the main baronial trouble-makers. It was constructed to an entirely new design, circular inside and polygonal outside, with a forebuilding and three rectangular turrets attached, from which flanking fire could cover all the main faces of the keep, and contained three storeys. As usual the entrance was to a large room in the second storey. There are an unusually large number of small rooms, including two kitchens, with sinks and flues, garderobes, and a cistern in the west turret. The well-shaft in the basement is provided with hand and foot holes built into the stonework. Orford was said to be Henry's favourite castle and other polygonal towers were built by his orders at Tickhill in the West Riding, where there are a few remains of the decagonal keep; at Chilham in Kent, where the octagonal structure has been modernized; and at Gisors (thirty-five miles south-east of Rouen by N14 and 14b) in Normandy, where Henry was accustomed to meet—and quarrel with—his perpetual adversary Louis VII.

Orford has been described as one of the most extraordinary keeps to be seen anywhere, but an even more remarkable one was erected about 1180 at Conisbrough (A630, Sheffield–Doncaster) by Henry's half-brother. Conisbrough carries the Orford design a stage further, embodying a number of improvements. Here both the interior and the exterior are cylindrical and from the latter there project six tremendous semi-hexagonal buttresses almost a hundred feet high. These buttresses, shaped like the teeth of an immense gear-wheel eliminate the weak rectangular corners of those at Orford and also provide a better field of fire. There is no forebuilding, but an uncluttered open space, overlooking and commanding the drawbridge. Internally, instead of a continuous spiral staircase which might be rushed, the stairs at Conisbrough are interrupted at every floor and begin again at a different place so that each presents a fresh problem to an attacking force. The upper levels of the buttresses are strictly functional, containing a chapel, oven, pigeon-loft and two water tanks.

Yet the future did not in fact lie with towers like Orford and Conisbrough. The castle at Framlingham (B1119, west off A12, Ipswich–Lowestoft), the property of Hugh Bigod, had been dismantled by Henry's orders in 1175. As soon as the King was safely dead, Hugh's son Roger bought back Framlingham and proceeded to construct a different type of castle. Here there is an impressive curtain wall, originally over forty feet high and eight feet thick, armed with no less than thirteen towers each 60 feet high. Other buildings such as the hall and chapel were built into the inside of the curtain wall and there was a strong gatehouse, but there was nothing which could be called a keep. It was this new pattern, seen at its best in Edward I's Welsh castles, which was to dominate the thirteenth century. The Norman keep had gone for ever.

Throughout the twelfth century the building, or rebuilding, of parish churches in the Romanesque style had continued unchecked, with apparently little reference to the ups and downs of the monarchy. In general big parish churches were, paradoxically, mainly confined to the smaller places, since the larger towns usually possessed several churches and in consequence each was likely to be relatively small. A great many churches or parts of churches survive from this time—far too many to list here. To do justice to what has survived would require a whole book to itself. Here I can only describe the most dramatic features of Anglo-Norman church art, and add a short selection of churches which are not mentioned elsewhere. Those in search of more are referred to the titles in Further Information at the end of this book. It is the details which are often of the greatest interest—wall-paintings, sculpture, and the scenes carved on fonts or tympana, the space above door lintels.

Probably most churches once possessed something in the way of wall-paintings, but today these have almost all gone and only about a dozen churches have anything much from the twelfth century. Puritan displeasure and casual whitewash have each played their part, but damp has perhaps been the main enemy, for these paintings were not true frescoes painted into the wet plaster, but were executed on the surface when it was dry. Their faint and faded attraction can be experienced at the following places:

Canterbury Cathedral: St Paul and the viper (Acts 28), in St Anselm's chapel in the crypt.

Chaldon (Surrey): B2031 west of Caterham; a good Last Judgement.

Claverley (Shropshire): south of A454, Bridgnorth–Wolverhampton; Virtues and Vices—or are they just knights?—fighting.

Clayton (Sussex): on A273 north of Brighton; the Last Judgement.

Copford (Essex): south of A12, Chelmsford–Colchester, and six miles from the latter; Christ in Majesty and Apostles, restored.

Hardham (Sussex): A29, nine miles south of Billingshurst; St George at Antioch (see p. 107), Adam and Eve.

Kempley (Gloucestershire): south-east of A449, midway between Ledbury and Ross; Christ in Majesty and Apostles.

Patcham (Sussex): northern outskirts of Brighton; the Last Judgement.

Sculpture on the other hand is fairly indestructible and much has survived. Carving now breaks out everywhere, around doors and windows, on corbels and capitals, along string courses and screens. In general, religious subjects are rarer than in France or Italy and their place is often taken by the warrior and the wandering entertainer, the signs of the Zodiac or a bestiary of fabulous animals—in fact all those figures that had so infuriated St Bernard of Clairvaux.

Two churches are in a class by themselves. In Wiltshire, Malmesbury Abbey—the burial place of King Athelstan—was rebuilt in Henry's reign. The monastic buildings have gone and the interior, apart from the nave arcading, was largely recon-

structed in the fourteenth century, but the southern porch has
survived, the best example of contemporary French influence.
Today it is recognized as a fine work of art, but this was not
always so. As recently as 1934 the main authority described it
as 'graceless'. Words fail one.

The outer doorway is made up of eight arcs, five of them
carved with geometric and floral patterns and three—the second,
fourth and sixth—containing 144 figures depicting the virtues
and vices and scenes from the Bible. These are good, but the
inner porch is even better. Above its doorway is Christ in
Majesty and on the side walls are the twelve Apostles. Carved *in
situ* into the stonework they sit, impassive and impressive, their
robes falling about them in abstract patterns, the most beautiful
Romanesque sculpture in England.

Equally remarkable, but completely insular, are the carvings
at Kilpeck: if Malmesbury is evidence of the civilizing influence
of French Romanesque, Kilpeck provides proof of the survival
of much earlier native patterns. The church stands on a minor
road to the east of A465 (Hereford–Abergavenny) about eight
miles south of Hereford. Here, in dark red sandstone that one
might have expected to weather badly, are sharp-cut figures in
three distinct styles which nevertheless co-exist quite happily.
Outside at the east end the corbel table is decorated with carvings showing Irish influence, crude, mysterious, and occasionally
obscene.

The most exciting work is on the south doorway, its columns
carved with warriors and dragons, intertwining with Scandinavian intensity to such effect that not a square inch is untouched yet the basic structure remains clear. The capitals show
the green man, a pagan head with branches sprouting from its
mouth—the wild huntsman, brother to those who were reported
in the *Anglo-Saxon Chronicle* to have been seen at Peterborough
"black and huge and hideous, riding on black horses and goats".
Above, in the tympanum, is a highly stylized tree of life. The
third group of carvings is within the church where, on either
side of the chancel arch, there are three figures, perhaps Apostles,
remote and peaceful, in a purely Saxon style.

In many churches the best carving is often over the door, or
around the font—the latter is not infrequently older than the

church in which it now stands. Twelfth-century fonts are said to be more common in England than in any other country, and they are particularly numerous in Gloucestershire, Lancashire, Northamptonshire and Sussex. Local workshops of carvers existed and some of these have been identified, notably one based on Herefordshire and flourishing around the middle of the century.

In general the earliest fonts take the form of cylinders or cubes, their surfaces relieved with carving, sometimes religious but often secular. Ones that I find particularly enjoyable include the following:

Castle Frome (Hereford): south of A4103, Worcester–Hereford, and about twelve miles from the latter; Christ's baptism, the water like a circular plate, and a jolly lion.

Chaddesley Corbett (Worcestershire): A448, Kidderminster–Bromsgrove; dragons' tails, knotted.

Eardisley (Hereford): A4111, six miles south of Kingston; the Harrowing of Hell, and two men fighting with spears.

Fincham (Norfolk): A1122, Swaffham–Downham, and about four miles from the latter; Adam and Eve, the Nativity and Baptism, and the Adoration of the Magi, like Victorian dolls.

Hook Norton (Oxford): north of A361, Chipping-Norton–Banbury; Adam and Eve, Sagittarius and Aquarius.

Luppitt (Devon): west of A303, Ilminster–Honiton and about six miles from the latter; one of the best, with deep-cut carvings showing, on one side, a two-headed dragon and on another a nail being enthusiastically hammered into a man's head—perhaps a reference to the song of Deborah (Judges, v, 24–7). Notice the lovely tent curtain on the right of this scene.

South Milton (Devon): west of A381, Kingsbridge–Salcombe; dancing girl, thought to be Salome, and bearded heads.

Thorpe Arnold (Leicestershire): A607, just north of Melton Mowbray; St Michael and a Scandinavian dragon from the Danelaw.

Toller Fratrum (Dorset): south of A356, Crewkerne–Dorchester, and about ten miles from the latter; very primitive men support the rim.

Topsham (Devon): A377, Exeter–Exmouth; a frightening animal.

West Haddon (Northants): A428, Northampton–Rugby, eight miles from the latter; the entry into Jerusalem, and the Baptism.

There is an unusual lead font at Dorchester in Oxfordshire, and there are seven fonts made of black marble from Tournai—four of them in Hampshire probably imported by way of Southampton, of which that at Winchester is the best—which are important, though I personally dislike them.

The other main location of twelfth-century work is the tympanum, the semi-circular space between the lintel and the arch of the doorway, which is often filled with carving. About 200 worked tympana can still be seen, the great majority dating from the years 1125–1200, and again they are particularly common in the west, the heaviest concentrations being in Dorset, Wiltshire, Gloucestershire and Hereford areas where the Saxon traditions lasted the longest. They cover a considerable range of subjects, sometimes religious, often secular, but always transformed by the artist into a dramatic experience.

Christ in Majesty, so general on the Continent, is less common here; there is a good example at Barfreston (west of A256, Dover–Sandwich). One of the most charming of all tympana is that at Bishopsteignton (A381, Newton Abbot–Teignmouth) where the Magi march briskly to the Adoration.

At quite a number of churches St Michael destroys the dragon; there is a rather Frenchified example at Moreton Valence (west of A38 and about eight miles south of Gloucester) and there are fierce struggles at Hoveringham (east of A612 halfway between Nottingham and Newark) and at Kingswinford on the western outskirts of Dudley. One that got away is the superb Scandinavian dragon at Uppington, south of A5 between Shrewsbury and Wellington.

Other monsters abound, for as T. S. R. Boase says, "the snapping jaws were never far behind men's heels"; at Barton Seagrave (A6 south of Kettering) a monster of indeterminate species cheerfully devours a man. Less alarming are the griffins at Leckhampstead (west of B4494 about eight miles north of Newbury), an attractive mermaid at Stow Longa (south of A604 between Huntingdon and Thrapston) and Sagittarius the Archer at Stoke-sub-Hamdon (A3088 seven miles west of Yeovil).

A number of tympana show a figure holding in either hand a wild beast. This was possibly a pre-Christian pattern originating in the Near East, which became attached with varying degrees of suitability to David and Samson. Two variations are particularly worth seeing. At Stretton Sugwas (A438, Hereford–Willersley) Samson fights with a single lion—one of the finest of all tympana—while at Charney Bassett (south of A420 Oxford–Faringdon) the design has been adapted to show Alexander the Great being carried through the air by two griffins attached to his throne.

An interesting group are those tympana depicting St George helping the Crusaders at Antioch. At the time of the First Crusade, in 1098, the Crusaders were besieged in the city. When their position seemed desperate they sallied out and found themselves able to destroy the Turkish army. It was reported that they owed this success—complete and unexpected—to the arrival of a force of angelic cavalry led by St George, and 'St George at Antioch' became a favourite subject with western artists. There are representations at, among other places, Brinsop (A480 a little west of Hereford) now inside the church; Damerham (B3078 west of Fordingbridge); Wakerley (west of A43, Kettering–Stamford, and about ten miles from the latter), and Fordington on the outskirts of Dorchester.

Finally, the tympanum at Pennington, close by Lymington in Hampshire, carries a runic inscription which says, firmly and succinctly, "Forbid into this church any trouble".

The following list of parish churches not mentioned elsewhere in this book does not pretend to be anything more than a personal choice of ones I have enjoyed, chosen to cover as many counties as possible and to include some obscure examples which might otherwise be missed. Such a list is grossly unfair and wildly unscientific and will—quite justly—arouse the fury of those who know how much has been left out. But they need no list.

Fingest (Buckinghamshire): north-west of Marlow and west of B482.
Stewkley (Buckinghamshire): B4032, west of Leighton Buzzard.
Great Salkeld (Cumberland): B6412, north-east of Penrith.
Melbourne (Derbyshire): A514, south of Derby. One of the finest.
Studland (Dorset): B3351, south-east of Wareham.
Rainham (Greater London): A13

Leominster (Hereford): A49, north of Hereford.
Hemel Hempstead (Hertfordshire): A41, north of Watford.
Brook (Kent): north of A20 and east of Ashford.
St Margaret's-at-Cliffe (Kent): B2058, north-east of Dover.
Castor (Northamptonshire): A47, west of Peterborough.
Milborne Port (Somerset): A30, east of Yeovil.
Tutbury (Staffordshire): A50, north of Burton-on-Trent.
Compton (Surrey): B3000, south-west of Guildford.
North Marden (Sussex): B2141, north of Chichester.
Old Shoreham (Sussex): between Worthing and Brighton.
Kirkby Lonsdale (Westmorland): A65, south of Kendal.
Warndon (Worcestershire): eastern outskirts of Worcester.
North Newbald (Yorkshire, East Riding): just east of A1034 and south of Market Weighton.
Adel (Yorkshire, West Riding): A660, northern outskirts of Leeds.
Birkin, West Riding: south-east of Selby and south of A63.
Brayton, West Riding: A19, southern outskirts of Selby.
Thorpe Salvin, West Riding: west of Workshop and south of A57.

At Iffley, in the southern part of Oxford, the church of St Mary the Virgin was built about the years 1175–82. It is a fine Romanesque church in its own right, with a particularly good west front, highly decorated with the traditional chevrons and beakheads. But it has another importance. It was probably the last significant English church to be built in the Romanesque style—the style of the Normans.

For the Norman age was coming to an end. When the cathedral at Canterbury was gutted by fire in 1174 it was rebuilt in the new fashion—that amalgam of French and English Gothic known as Early English which was to mark the thirteenth century. The Norman semi-circular arch gave way to the narrow lancet window and the pointed vault at much the same date that the Norman keep was being superseded by new styles of fortification. And at this time also the crown passed from the half-Norman Henry II to men in whom the blood of Anjou and Aquitaine preponderated.

In 1189 Philip Augustus, that hard-headed King of France who knew so well how to profit from the self-destructive quarrels of the faithless Angevins, joined forces with Henry's eldest son

Richard. When the King of England heard the news he made no effort to raise an army, but instead retired silently to Chinon in his old homeland of Anjou. On 4th July, ill of blood-poisoning from a wound in his heel, Henry rode twenty miles to make his submission to the French king, whom he met at Villandry. As he gave Richard the stipulated kiss of peace the old temper flared briefly—"God grant that I may not die till I have had my revenge on you." But it was only a momentary flash. Nor was his prayer answered, for Henry died in agony at Chinon two days later. His servants at once stole everything on which they could lay their hands, even his clothes.

Richard succeeded to the throne. An absentee landlord, he spent less time in England than any other king—six months in all. His first act was to release Eleanor, who had spent the last seventeen years under house arrest. The indomitable old mischief-maker commented "prisons are irksome, it is a most delightful refreshment to the soul to come out". She lived on for another fifteen years, dying at last in 1204 aged over eighty. By then John, the last of the Angevins, was King and attempting to continue his father's policy. One can understand why he was the latter's favourite son—he was the only one who understood what Henry II had tried to do.

Henry II's body had been taken to the abbey of Fontevrault, close to Saumur on the borders of Anjou and Poitou, where his tomb can still be seen. The abbey has had a chequered history, having been used in later times as both a barracks and a prison, but today the nave stands impressively large and bare, except for four tombs. The draped effigies are those of John's wife Isabella of Angoulême, of King Henry II—and of Eleanor and Richard, who between them had bedevilled his reign.

GLOSSARY

Ambulatory	aisle round the apse
Apse	semi-circular end of a chancel or chapel
Arcade	line of arches. A blind arcade is attached to a wall
Buttress	projecting support to strengthen a wall
Capital	carved stone at the head of a shaft
Clerestory	upper storey of the nave walls, pierced by windows
Corbel table	row of projecting stones, occurring just below the eaves, usually externally
Crossing	space where the east-west line of a church is crossed by the transepts
Lintel	horizontal stone above an opening
Moulding	decoration of masonry
Narthex	vestibule at the main, usually west, entrance to a church
Presbytery	east part of church beyond the choir, containing the High Altar and reserved to the clergy
Quoins	dressed stones at the angles of a building
Rood	cross or crucifix
String course	continuous horizontal moulding projecting from the face of a wall
Triforium	gallery or arcade above the nave arches and below the clerestory windows
Tympanum	space over a doorway between the lintel and the arch

FURTHER INFORMATION
(INCLUDING BIBLIOGRAPHY)

The Ordnance Survey publishes the following specialized maps:
1. *Ancient Britain. A map of the major visible antiquities of Great Britain older than A.D. 1066*, on a scale of approximately ten miles to one inch and in two parts, the south sheet covering England and Wales as far north as Scarborough; the remainder of England and the whole of Scotland are on the companion north sheet.
2. *Britain in the Dark Ages*, on a scale of sixteen miles to one inch and including a useful introduction, which covers the period between the end of Roman rule and the time of King Alfred (410–870).
3. *Britain before the Norman Conquest*, on a scale of ten miles to one inch. This is in effect a book containing an outline of the period 870–1066 together with a map of Great Britain in two sheets.

The guides to individual sites produced by the Department of the Environment are invaluable and can usually be bought on the spot. At present the opening hours for most of the sites under its care are as follows:

	Weekdays	Sundays
March–April, October	09.30–17.30	14.00–17.30
May–September	09.30–19.00	14.00–19.00
November–February	09.30–16.00	14.00–16.00

The Council for British Archaeology, 8 St Andrew's Place, London N.W.1, publish lists of sites at which excavation is taking place, at many of which assistance is welcome. A journal which is designed to appeal also to the non-professional is *Current Archaeology*, obtainable direct from the Editors, 9 Nassington Road, London N.W.3.

The National Trust publishes *The What To See Atlas*, a great deal more useful than its title suggests and not confined to Trust properties.

Translations easily available include:

Beowulf, transl. D. Wright (Penguin, 1957)

Bede, *A History of the English Church and People*, transl. L. Sherley-Price (Penguin, 1955)

The Anglo-Saxon Chronicle, transl. G. N. Garmonsway (Dent, 1954)

English Historical Documents, Vol I, ed. D. Whitelock (Eyre and Spottiswoode, 1954)

There are plenty of general histories. Four different approaches to the Saxon period are provided by:

P. Hunter Blair, *An Introduction to Anglo-Saxon England* (Cambridge, 1956)

H. P. R. Finberg, *The Formation of England, 550–1042* (Hart-Davis, 1974)

Sir Frank Stenton, *Anglo-Saxon England* (Oxford, 3rd edition, 1970)

D. M. Wilson, *The Anglo-Saxons* (Penguin, 1971)

Works covering the twelfth century include:

A. L. Poole, *From Domesday Book to Magna Carta* (Oxford, 2nd edition, 1958)

D. M. Stenton, *English Society in the Early Middle Ages* (Penguin, 1951)

The relevant volumes in the series *Kings and Queens of England* ed. Lady Antonia Fraser (Weidenfeld and Nicolson) are splendidly illustrated.

Some valuable general surveys of art and architecture are:

D. Talbot-Rice, *English Art, 871–1100* (Oxford, 1952)

T. S. R. Boase, *English Art, 1100–1216* (Oxford, 1953)

A. W. Clapham, *English Romanesque Architecture before the Norman Conquest* (Oxford, 1930), and *English Romanesque Architecture after the Norman Conquest* (Oxford, 1934)

H. M. and J. Taylor, *Anglo-Saxon Architecture*, 2 vols, (Cambridge, 1965)

R. Stoll, *Architecture and Sculpture in Early Britain* (Thames and Hudson, 1967)

FURTHER INFORMATION (AND BIBLIOGRAPHY)

For specific information on castles try:

H. M. Colvin, *The History of the King's Works*, Vols I and II, *The Middle Ages* (H.M.S.O., 1963)

B. H. St. J. O'Neil, *Castles* (H.M.S.O., 1953)

D. F. Renn, *Norman Castles in Britain* (Baker, 1968)

S. Toy, *The Castles of Great Britain* (Heinemann, 4th edition, 1966)

For cathedrals:

G. H. Cook, *The English Cathedral through the Centuries* (Phoenix, 1957)

For monasteries:

R. G. Beer, *Abbeys* (H.M.S.O., 1959)

G. H. Cook, *English Monasteries in the Middle Ages* (Phoenix, 1961)

D. Knowles and J. K. St Joseph, *Monastic Sites from the Air* (Cambridge, 1952)

For parish churches:

Sir John Betjeman, *Guide to English Parish Churches* (Collins, 1958)

Books dealing with specific topics include:

L. Alcock, *Arthur's Britain* (Penguin, 1973)

F. Bond, *Fonts and Font Covers* (Oxford, 1908)

R. L. S. Bruce-Mitford, *The Sutton Hoo Ship Burial* (British Museum, 1968)

Sir Cyril Fox, *Offa's Dyke* (Oxford, 1955)

C. E. Keyser, *A List of Norman Tympana and Lintels* (Elliot Stock, 1927)

Sir Frank Stenton, *The Bayeux Tapestry* (Phaidon, 1957)

G. Zarnecki, *English Romanesque Sculpture, 1066–1140* (Tiranti, 1951) and *Later English Romanesque Sculpture, 1140–1210* (Tiranti, 1953)

R. W. V. Elliott, *Runes* (Manchester University Press, 1959)

INDEX OF SITES

M

Incidental references to all the above sites are, where appropriate, included in the General Index.

GENERAL INDEX

A

Abbeville, 95
Abernethy, 101
Adelard of Bath, 129
Aelfric, 73
Aethelhere, King, 31
Agriculture, 74–5
Aidan, St, 37
Aislabie, John, 149
Alcuin, 47
Alnwick, 154
Alfred, King, 62–5, 67
Ambazac, 132
Ambrosius Aurelianus, 17
Animals, farm, 75
Anglo-Saxon Chronicle, 17, 29–
    30, 60, 72, 90, 101, 103, 104,
    108, 133, 165
Architects, 112
Arms and armour, 76–8, 107
Arthur, 'King', 17, 26–7
Athelney, 62–3
Athelstan, King, 41, 65, 72, 74,
    79–80, 164
Augustine, St, 37, 51
Augustinians, 140–41

B

Badbury, 17
Badon, Mount, 17
Bailey, 108
Bamburgh, 33
Barbury Castle, 18
Bath, 17, 18, 34, 70
Battle Abbey, 145, 147
Bayeux Tapestry, 94, 96–7,
    108–09
Beaulieu, 147
Bec, 132
Becca Banks, 21
Becket, Thomas, 141, 151–52

Bede, St, 30, 34–5, 37, 41–3, 51,
    53, 60, 120
Bell-towers, 82, 84
Benedictines, 138–39
Benedictional of St Ethelwold, 72
Benty Grange, 77
Beowulf, 32
Bernard, St, 143–44, 164
Bernay, 115
Bernicia, 33
Bertha, Queen, 51
Bewcastle cross, 49–50
Bigod, Hugh and Roger, 162
Bookland, 81
Born, Bertran de, 155
Bows, 77–8
Bridges, 70, 74, 76
British kingdoms, 18–28
Brown, 'Capability', 149
Brunnanburgh, 79
Building, methods of, 112,
    116–18
Burghal Hidage, 67–8
Burhs, 67–9
Burials:
    Celtic, 22–5
    Saxon 28–9
    Scandinavian, 87–8
Bury St Edmunds, 154

C

Cadwallon, 36
Caen, 99–100, 113, 115
Cambridge, University Library,
    42
Camden, William, 49
Camelot, 26–7
Canons, 140–41
Canute, *see* Cnut
Cardiff, 101, 128, 138
Carlisle, 70, 104

181